"In a culture obsessed wit[...] pyramid upside down, prov[...] New Testament really has to say about the subject."

Frank Viola
Author of *Reimagining Church, From Eternity to Here,* and *Revise Us Again*
www.frankviola.org

"Take a moment and notice the growing disenchantment with leadership idolatry in this country. Then let Lance Ford be your guide through the massive changes God is working among us in this regard. *UnLeader* is a fast, engaging read that makes a compelling case for a different way—a starkly biblical way—toward leading the church into God's future."

David Fitch
Pastor, Author of *Prodigal Christianity: 10 Signposts to the Missional Frontier*
B R Lindner Chair of Evangelical Theology
Northern Seminary

"As the church struggles through seizmic shifts, *UnLeader* unwraps the reality of true God-sized influence. The future of the church and the fate of the world, at least in your neighborhood, are at stake . . . so read only if you intend to give your life away."

Hugh Halter
Author of *The Tangible Kingdom* and *Sacrilege*

"Careful, this book is dangerous. It rips the Band-Aid off a festering wound exposing much that is wrong with the church in America; then applies the salve of Jesus' kingdom paradigm, which can bring healing, health, and fruitfulness. Many dynamic leaders in Christendom will not like this book and will prefer that you do not read it . . . that's why you should read it."

Neil Cole
Founding catalyst of the organic church movement and author of many books, including *Organic Church, Organic Leadership, Church 3.0, Journeys to Significance,* and *Church Transfusion*

"Lance has called out the 800-pound gorilla. In *UnLeader* he shouts: 'You are naked!' to those who in their mind are strutting their finest stuff. Thankfully he is not talking to me, but should you wonder if he has you in mind, ask some people around you. Then fire them if you don't like what you hear."

Reggie McNeal
Best-selling author of *The Present Future* and *Missional Renaissance*

"There is such wonderful excitement about change needed in the church with a renewed and passionate focus on mission and 'disciples not just decisions' being made. So these are very, very encouraging days for the church. However, in addition to God's Spirit empowering us, what will take all these great thoughts about what is needed in the church to be done and turn it into reality is leadership. But if we repeat the same leadership philosophies of the past, we will only repeat what we have learned not to do. Lance Ford doesn't rehash leadership of the past but explores leadership of the future. And not just leadership but leadership for those who are desiring change in the church for the sake of mission. This is why *UnLeader* is such an inspiring book, as it is based on what we need to be 'unleading' for the church on mission in today's very different world from the past."

Dan Kimball
Author of *Adventures in Churchland*
On staff at Vintage Faith Church and George Fox University

"For the churches to remain healthy, we need to continue to listen to the prophetic voices in our midst. Lance Ford's book will challenge, but also inform you. It will give you much to consider as you seek to grow leaders who look like Jesus."

Mike Breen
Founder Global Team Leader 3DM

"There is an elephant in the middle of the room of the American church. It is the destructive obsession with business models of leadership that have displaced the ways of Jesus and are keeping the church from being the transformative force it was intended to be. In *UnLeader*, Lance Ford calls it for what it is and offers a clear way out of the insanity. This book has the real potential to set a greatly needed course correction for the church, if only people will accept the challenge to read it and have the courage to actually do what it says."

Brad Brisco
Co-author of *Missional Essentials*

"In the missional conversation the last bastille of Christendom to be challenged is leadership. It seems the imagination of the people of God in the context of mission has been unleashed; however, we often still default to old paradigms of leadership. Lance in his book *UnLeader*, address these issues head on. A confronting read for all those who serve in the church. Lance is unafraid to tackle the hard and taboo topics in the leadership arena. I would love every person who goes through Forge to wrestle honestly about this topic and *UnLeader* gives the platform for this discussion. Some people may find it a hard critic; however, Lance's heart is to champion all those who have been burnt and hurt by wrong leadership, reimagine a biblical description of leadership and to honor Jesus, the greatest example of a servant leader."

Kim Hammond
National Director of Forge America and the Director of Missional Imagination for Community Christian Church/The New Thing Network

FUN LEADER

UN LEADER

LANCE FORD

REIMAGINING LEADERSHIP
. . . AND WHY WE MUST

BEACON HILL PRESS
OF KANSAS CITY

Library of Congress Cataloging-in-Publication Data
Ford, Lance, 1964-
  Unleader : reimagining leadership—and why we must / Lance Ford.
    p. cm.
  Includes bibliographical references.
  ISBN 978-0-8341-2885-9 (pbk.)
  1. Leadership—Religious aspects—Christianity. 2. Christian leadership. I. Title.
  BV4597.53.L43F67 2012
  248.4—dc23

                                                                    2012020361

10 9 8 7 6 5 4 3 2 1

To the unleaders
who have most shaped my life:
Sam Spence, Tri Robinson, George Wilson,
Royce Thomas, and Jordan Ford

CONTENTS

FOREWORD

This is a hard-hitting book—no doubt about it. In these pages my mate Lance does not hold back in giving what he calls "leaderdom" a thoroughly scathing, but nonetheless profoundly prophetic, serve. Clearly he does not jive with the leadership cult that is celebrated in many churches throughout the land. His aim in writing this book is to call leaders to thoroughly assess who they are in the Lord (they are followers) and how they are being perceived by others in the church and out (they are witnesses). *Thankfully,* the book is laced with a consistent call for leaders to live a life that is more consistent with our Lord and Master, Jesus Christ. I believe that if it were not for this distinctly Christ-shaped vision of leadership that undergirds and guides the critique, *UnLeader* would be an unremittingly hard pill for most to swallow.

I must admit to have been increasingly concerned with the culture of celebrity that surrounds the adulation of many popular Christian leaders in the West. Aside from the contrived "heroism" that is embodied in such forms of leadership, to my eyes it looks as if it is an illegitimate attempt to steal glory from Jesus himself. The celebrity is a mere slave to the crowd. He or she needs the crowd as much as the crowd longs for a celebrity. But this is not Christian leadership; it is way too codependent to be viewed as an extension of discipleship—that is, adherence to Jesus. Clearly Jesus himself, while willingly serving the people, was never subservient to the consumerist groupthink of the undiscipled crowd—and neither were any of our great saints and heroes, such as Paul, Augustine, Patrick, Francis, Bonhoeffer, and Martin Luther King Jr. This marks them as different from the false heroisms of our day.

The second phrase in the Lord's Prayer affirms that God's name (representing all that he is and signifies) is to be made holy (hallowed) through the obedient actions of his people in every area of their lives. In other words, in the biblical worldview, God's name is hallowed when I do things that cause others to honor and respect God and all that he is to the world. To hallow his name is thus the highest ethical act we can do as believers; it is to bring glory to the One we love through the things we do. It is not hard to see that it lies at the heart of worship itself. Our lives must point beyond ourselves to the life of the One we serve. This is the very meaning of Christlikeness. It also lies at the heart of the whole biblical notion of being a *witness*. The quality of our lives *does* matter; that is, people read the message of our lives and God's reputation is somehow bound up with it.

But implied in this call to hallow God's name is also the possibility of its opposite, what the rabbis call "blaspheming the Name." To blaspheme God's name is to distort its meaning in the world so that the character and purposes of God are obscured, his glory veiled, and his name cursed by others because of what we *as his witnesses* do. Blasphemy inverts holiness and makes it inaccessible to others. Our lives can therefore either hallow *or* blaspheme God's name. In short, it fundamentally means bearing false witness. This is a horror to all who love God truly.

Leaders, those people whose actions are amplified because of their influence on others, more than anything else are required to live a consistent life worthy of the Name they represent. If they are not doing this, their acts distort (also in an amplified way) the nature and meaning of the gospel itself. God gets the blame when we get it wrong!

Viewed as such, Christian celebrity, with its potential to becoming an ideological cult of self-promotion, can distort what Jesus essentially stands for and amount to bearing false witness. As someone who is involved in many of the forums that could so easily lend themselves to the cultivation of such celebrity, along with its false representation of leadership, I have to admit that I can discern in myself a slow but inexorable slide toward pride and conceit. I need to be constantly addressed by the gospel, called to account by Lord and community, to repent and continually surrender myself to the call to be an adoring follower of the One who won my salvation through culturally ignominious means—a life of suffering love and a death on a cross.

UnLeader is a call for honest discernment: Am I a true disciple? Am I really becoming more and more like the One I claim to follow? Does my life reflect the quality of the One I love? Or do I fundamentally bear false witness to him and so damage his cause? Am I becoming a narcissist, in love with my own image in the face of my adoring fans, or am I being a leader as Jesus intended me to be? The reader is called to submit himself or herself to such probing questions. If *UnLeader* does contain a prophetic challenge, and I do personally believe it does, then, like all prophetic texts, we ignore it to our peril.

—Alan Hirsch
Founder of Forge Mission Training Network
Co-leader of Future Travelers

FUN LEADER

PART I
ABANDONING LEADERSHIP

*Jesus called them to him and said,
"You know that the rulers of the
Gentiles lord it over them, and their
great ones exercise authority
over them. It shall not
be so among you."*
—Matt. 20:25-26a

INTRODUCTION
NOT SO AMONG YOU

I'm trying to free your mind, Neo. But I can only show you
the door. You're the one that has to walk through it.

—Morpheus, *The Matrix*[1]

Don't let anyone capture you with empty philosophies and
high-sounding nonsense that come from human thinking and
from the spiritual powers of this world, rather than from
Christ.

—Col. 2:8 (NLT)

S top the insanity!" If you were of television-watching age in the 1990s, you will remember this phrase. It is from an infomercial that blasted off with a fast-paced collage of headlines from diet makers and purveyors of weight-loss programs blitzing the screen. Suddenly the picture would freeze-frame and Susan Powter, an annoyingly energetic buzz-cut blonde, would appear waving her arms and screaming into the camera, "Stop the insanity!" Her talking point or, rather, screaming point was that diets don't work. They are mere stopgaps that are not sustainable over the long haul. A lifestyle change is what it takes to be fit and healthy.

Recently I spoke at a gathering of denominational leaders for a two-day symposium on church leadership. As I listened to a young Southern California pastor build his talk, launched from a "leadership lesson" gleaned from former New York mayor Rudy Giuliani, I finally had to dismiss myself to keep from shouting Susan Powter's famous line and summarily getting myself invited to leave.

When will we recognize where the leadership language and practices of politics and business lead? When will we cease looking to the fallen system of a fallen culture for ideas and methods of operating within the kingdom of the risen Savior? Does Attila the Hun really have something to contribute along-side the words of Jesus and the apostles Paul, Peter, and John? Does Apple founder Steve Jobs and Starbucks guru Howard Schultz have something we are lacking in order to effectively move forward into the kingdom of heaven? Are we so dull of hearing the voices of the Father, Son, and Holy Spirit that we need the voices of Wharton, Harvard, and Wall Street?

Every which way we turn, a seemingly endless volley of leadership-centric conversations dominates the contemporary evangelical church scene. Such material is not hard to find. In fact, it is impossible to avoid if you are a pastor or member of a church staff. Over the past two decades the subject of leadership has steamrolled to the point that it now effectively captivates the hearts and imaginations of most folks whom God has given responsibility as servants for the body of Christ. Ask around and you will find that leadership issues are perceived as *the* primary burden and missing link, the greatest need in the church today. Our minds are soaked with the belief that "everything rises or falls on leadership." This is so much the case that I have a hunch some church leaders are sure this phrase is from the Bible.

The drumbeat is that what is needed to solve most of our church problems is more and better leadership. Compounding this is the idea that most leadership styles and principles, if they are considered "successful and productive," are transferable to the kingdom of God and useful for the church. The mind-set is that if it worked for John "Neutron Jack" Welch and General Electric, it will work for the church. If Harvard Business School concludes that certain leadership principles are a road to success, by all means sign me up. Learn from this or that Fortune 500 executive and your church can also go from *good to great*.

The largest church leadership conferences each year include talks from corporate-business stars and world famous CEOs who make no claim to be followers of Christ. The bookshelves of most pastors and church leaders are filled with solid collections of *New York Times* best-selling books on leadership, authored by corporate-business gurus and political figures. Furthermore, twice as many books on Christian leadership are available at Amazon.com as compared to titles on discipleship. Leadership making has not only trumped disciple making but also trampled it and left it in the dust. Regarding *servantship*, look for books on it and you are up the proverbial creek without a paddle. I have not found one Christian book on serving as a coveted position in and of itself. When they do get close to it, authors in the Christian leadership field (in my research) cannot help themselves but to use the phrase "servant-leader." "Leader" seems always to get squeezed in. Mere "servantship" is not considered enough.

Perhaps the biggest mix-up concerning the current leadership obsession is that Jesus himself directly contradicts much—if not most—of what is being imported into the church under the leadership mantra. Better put, much of it is expressly forbidden by Jesus. Can you imagine the apostle Paul hosting a leadership conference for the early church with a lineup of speakers such as Roman governor Gaius Suetonius Paulinus; Revolutionary leader Simon bar Giora; and John Philip Maximus, owner of the Roman Traders Market (I made up this last guy)? Ridiculous, huh?

Most disconcerting is that Jesus himself is not our first choice as our model for leadership. When the character and person of Jesus are washed out through so-called strategic initiatives and sound leadership decisions, a clash of kingdoms has occurred. And in large part these are the coordinates being followed by most pastors in today's evangelical church circles.

This book is not about eliminating leadership in the church. Far from that, it is about redefining and recalibrating leadership according to "Jesusian" coordinates. To borrow a phrase from my Aussie mates, "What am I on about?" It is to say that the only acceptable leadership moves we make in the church must be made by following Jesus himself. If you are stepping off the path of following Jesus in your leadership methods and means, you are not followable yourself. You may be quick-witted, smooth-tongued, and a strategizing whiz kid, but if you use those skills in contradiction to the person of Jesus, your way of leadership is not worth following.

Leadership in the church involves hard decisions, but if the way you carry out those hard decisions is not saturated with meekness, gentleness, kindness, peace, and patience, then your leadership is shipwrecked. You don't deserve to be followed. The only leaders worthy of being followed in the body of Christ are the ones who are following Christ himself—his ways and means.

It is time we give Jesus credit and agree with Dallas Willard's proclamation that Jesus was the smartest person ever to live. The message emanating from his kingdom consistently did and does contradict the ways and means of the kingdoms of this world. His message downright confounds the kingdoms of this world and scandalizes our most common sensibilities and intuitive responses. Jesus' way of leading flatly does not make sense.

In our search for a way of leading that does seem sensible, we have drifted into the weeds of human ways, words, and will. Along the leadership way we have lost the servantship way—Jesus, *the* Way. We have exchanged *the* Truth, Jesus himself, for falsehoods. And in trying to secure a successful life for our churches and ourselves we have missed *the* Life, Jesus himself. If you want to help me be a better leader, if you want to help my church in her pursuit of faithfulness to God, then teach me servantship by teaching me how to follow Jesus.

Take me to someone who is following Jesus with his or her character, as evidenced in his or her methods. Take me to someone who is following Jesus in meekness and servanthood. Take me to someone who has the guts to risk reputation, stature, fame, and notoriety for the sake of pointing the spotlight on Jesus. Want me to journey with you, on your team, with your church? Please, take me to your server, not your leader.

This book has two parts. The impetus for it comes from a gospel passage that is quite familiar to most pastors and leaders, yet receives much neglect in actual obedience in the real world. In short, we read what Jesus said about leadership, ignore his commandments, and move on, doing things our own way. My hope is that by camping in this passage and letting what Jesus said penetrate our heads and hearts, we will change not only what leadership means to us in the kingdom of God but also how we lead our churches and ministries in the future. The first half of this book will give attention to the first half of this passage:

> But Jesus called them to him and said, "You know that the rulers of the Gentiles lord it over them, and their great ones exercise authority over them. It shall not be so among you. But whoever would be great among you must be your ser-

vant, and whoever would be first among you must be your slave, even as the Son of Man came not to be served but to serve, and to give his life as a ransom for many. (Matt. 20:25-28)

We will unpack what Jesus wanted to convey as it relates to the twenty-first-century church. What does "the rulers of the Gentiles lord it over" mean for us today? How is that manifesting in our churches? What does that look like? What does the "great ones exercise authority over" mean for us today? We will encounter Jesus' statement "It shall not be so among you" and seek to confront the ways we have ignored him. We will ask and answer the question, "In what ways is 'it so' among us?"

In the second half of the book we will move to the second half of the passage. Our attention will center on what it means to be a servant in the kingdom of God and how we can ensure our churches are servant-centric cultures. The servant metaphor has fallen short in capturing our imagination. On the surface it lacks excitement. When given the choice of being a leader or a servant, the choice for the flesh is obvious. Would you rather be the CEO of a Fortune 500 company or would you prefer to be that person's butler or maid? Who wants to attend seminars on operating laundry services, foot washing, and floor scrubbing when they can learn about vision casting, strategic initiatives, and personal development? Nevertheless, following Jesus into the place of servantship is the call that is on the lives of citizens of the kingdom of God.

Jesus told his disciples he wanted them to abandon the leadership culture of the kingdoms of the world and follow him into the servantship culture of the kingdom of God. He will have it no other way. His requirement is that we lay down the crown and scepter of leadership and pick up the towel and basin of servantship. To be a true servant for Christ means we must become an unleader.

ONE

LEADEROHOLISM
THE ADDICTIVE OBSESSION

Why are we so infatuated with leadership? Why is following
so disagreeable to us?

—Scott Bessenecker[1]

It wasn't until I began to try and understand life and
organizations from a follower perspective that I noticed
the overt negative bias toward followers in the leadership
literature.

—Rusty Ricketson[2]

For me there is just something about the smell of a book. Old or new—it really doesn't matter. I've considered the possibility that I need therapy, because the scent of a book could be regarded as a bit of a fetish with me. When I am reading a book, every once and a while I can't help but to hold it to my nose to catch a whiff of its aroma. For the longest time I said I would never own an electronic reader until one was invented that could emit a book scent. One day I even began wondering if there were other people out there like me. Could it be that someone had created a cologne or perfume that smelled like a book? I did an online search, and sure enough there is a fragrance on the market that claims to smell like a library. So I guess I'm not the only one out here that needs counseling.

For over twenty years one of my favorite places to while away a day is at Steel's, a Kansas City treasure trove of used Christian books. The entire place smells like one giant book. I love to spend a cold winter's day in this floor-to-ceiling, wall-to-wall maze of used Christian books. One day as I warmed my hands around a still steaming hot latte while strolling among the books at Steel's, I had a thought: "I wonder how many books they have on the subject of leadership and how that number compares with the number of books on the subject of discipleship and disciple making." Seminary libraries and well-stocked Christian bookstores can tell us a lot about variations in theology and the overall history of Christianity, along with trends and fads that have moved in and out of the faith through the ages. I found my way to the leadership section to conduct a survey.

There were so many books on Christian leadership that I had to take a couple of steps back from the large wall of a half dozen or more seven-foot-tall, five-foot-wide shelves holding them to view them all. I really wasn't too surprised that there were so many books on leadership. After all, there were seventy thousand books in the store. It was to be expected. The surprise came when I moved to the section that contained the discipleship books. Stepping back wasn't necessary this time. Discipleship as a subject matter required less than one shelf to contain the volumes. This meant that for every book on disciple making there were about ten books on leadership. I was disappointed but not surprised. I knew this was not a case of supply giving way to demand.

I have been around the publishing scene enough to know that most Christian publishers, though they are in the industry because of their love for Christ and the kingdom of God, print most of their books based not on what they deem the readership needs but on what they figure readers *want*. They can't sell what people won't buy. In fact, this book you are reading right now was passed over by one publisher who told me, "Lance, you are right about what is needed here, but pastors don't want to hear about following or serving; they're interested in how to be leaders." I answered, "Precisely—thus the need for the book."

THE LEADERSHIP COCKTAIL

We need a leadership sobriety checkpoint. We must sober up. There is a drinking problem in the church today. What we are about to delve into in the coming pages and chapters of this book is not meant as spear throwing and criticism for mere criticism's sake. This is more of an intervention. Those of us who are questioning the most prominent contemporary church leadership practices may be looked at as nothing more than behind the times or prudish, dismissed as mere critics. That is not the aim here—far from it. I just happen to believe friends shouldn't let friends lead churches (while) drunk.

Leadership could be justifiably called an addictive obsession in the church today. Attendance at church-planting and leadership conferences swell into the thousands, with attendees hanging on every leadership nugget, hoping to gain an edge from leadership gurus that dip cupfuls of church growth punch, spiked with shots of leadership greatness. Pastors and church planters leave the gatherings loaded with books and binders, staggering out to put into practice the methods of the experts, in hopes of developing the next gigachurch. Blogs and leadership-soaked websites clog the Internet with article after article, pithy quote after pithy quote being tweeted and facebooked by the thousands every day.

Over the last two decades in particular we have witnessed the rise of the superstar church leader—the skilled preacher who is also a world-class CEO type—possessing the ability to attract and inspire followers and build a great organization. The predominant leadership patterns of the twenty-first-century church have been cut from the forms and models of rainmakers, larger-than-life personalities who are gifted with the capacity to paint a compelling picture of a preferred future along with the acumen to bring that future into reality. Some church leaders have even given titles to themselves that promote this skill, calling themselves futurists, culture guides, architects of transformation, and so on. Whatever happened to the good ole apostles, prophets, and evangelists?

I am convinced that the overwhelming majority of pastors and leaders that are addicted to leadership are deeply sincere in their love for Jesus and the cause of the kingdom of God. The problem is that the punch has been spiked! And it is past time we recognize it, analyze it, throw it out, and go back to the original ingredients. Several factors or beliefs make up the recipe I call the leadership cocktail, the drink of choice for the vast majority of current evangelical pastors and church staff members. These ingredients include a handful of ideologies that are passively chugged down without questioning their source or the possibility that they induce a stupor that is often in direct opposition to the clearly stated commands of Jesus and the authors of the New Testament Epistles.

Sometimes we just need to laugh at ourselves in order to not just sit and cry. I have very few friends who are in vocational ministry that have not been caught up in the grip of leaderoholism at one time or another. I'm not here to throw stones, because it was certainly my addiction and I will rat myself out in the pages to come. Brant Hansen wrote a series of blogs that parodied the obsession with leadership among church leaders. He called it *The 417 Rules of Awesomely Bold Leadership*, and it is written from his alter ego, Brant Hansen, Vision Coach. Here are a couple of his posts:

Rule #281:
What's More Challenging to Lead: A Church, or a Business, or the Military? Actually, They're <u>Exactly</u> the Same
Here's the point: I'm often asked, because I teach leadership to church AND business leaders AND military generals, using the same exact principles, "What's more challenging?" And the answer is that it's exactly the same. As the kids say these days, "Duh!" friend! (I smile as I write that!) *All take awesomeness. All take boldness.* All take gutsy decisions and command presence. All require looking to the future, seeing and seizing the trends. All demand a leader who sorta listens, but then calls the shots, and tells people what to do, because the buck stops here. And like Patton said, "A good plan, violently executed now, is better than a perfect plan next week," and that's true on the battlefield, in the boardroom, or at V.B.S. *Obviously, all leadership principles apply to everyone, everywhere, regardless of context.* That's what's so awesome about it. I was explaining this while tandem-biking through Texas with Brett Favre, and . . .[3]

Rule #114:
There's only one way Leadership gets done: *Through talking about leading.*
[Excerpt]
. . . and I'm here to tell you, that next morning I woke up with sixteen more rules and twelve more acronyms! My publisher was thrilled to get the manuscript on time, again. *Leadership is all about coming through in the clutch.* And you can't just "get" leadership. <u>You have to live it.</u> And how do you "live it"? Good question, friend! Here's how: *You travel around and talk about it.* Endlessly. Traveling around, talk-

ing about it, writing about it, coming up with rules about it, rhyming it with other words, googling for quotes about it, putting those quotes on notecards, and updating your books with the things that you wrote on those notecards. I, the Vision Coach, a true leader? Well, friend, sometimes I can barely get out the door in the morning. Why? Friend, I'm pinned in by stacks of thousands of notecards.

. . . yes, I'm a leader. **Leadership is talking about leadership.** It's like my friend says, who met Tiger Woods: "Simply hanging around with golfers doesn't make you a golfer." No. But traveling the world, yammering on about golfing, without pause, for decades? Now you're golfing, friend![4]

JUST A SERVANT

When was the last time you heard of a conference on followership or servantship? I am pretty sure I have never heard of one. Or when have you ever heard of someone described as a great servant or a great follower? Who wants to be one of those? There is just nothing compelling about those prospects. The idea of following or serving has no pizzazz. After all, we know that *anyone* can be a follower. And waiting tables is what people do in the early stages of trying to make it to the top.

The attention is all on becoming a leader, then becoming a better leader, and then becoming a leader of leaders. Leadership is the subject deemed to be most important in the business culture and in contemporary church culture. Leadership education and development has become a $50 billion[5] industry in itself. But the idea of being labeled as a follower or servant is a derisive thought to most people. Think of the many times you have heard someone issue the challenge by asking, "Are you a leader or a follower?" To accept the label "follower" is perceived as giving up—an immediate surrender and abandonment of the possibility for greatness or of living up to one's full potential. Many times I have been in on conversations where someone assesses another person's capabilities, dismissing that person from consideration for a particular invitation or promotion with the phrase, "He [or She] is a follower, not a leader." It is as if servants or followers are a dime a dozen.

Author Barbara Kellerman says,

Leadership expert John Gardner so disliked the word *follower* that he chose simply not to use it. "The connotations of the word 'follower' suggest too much passivity and dependence to make it a fit term for those who are at the other end of the dialogue with leaders," Gardner wrote. "For this reason I shall make frequent use of the word 'constituent.'"[6]

Though Jesus obviously thought highly of the idea of following—using it in his invitation, "Follow me" (Matt. 16:24)—it is virtually detested today. Sure, followers are necessary to build a great church, but you would never want to be one yourself. Followership advocate Robert Kelley writes,

The negative followership myth has its roots in Social Darwinism. "Survival of the fittest" pits contenders against one another like the ancient Greek gods who battled one another. To struggle and compete is natural, good, and right. The winners, by definition, are leaders; the losers are everyone else. The Darwinistic viewpoint has infused culturally charged values into the terms "follower" and "leader." It also created a false, hierarchical topography, as if only leaders matter while the remaining 90 to 99 percent of the world is inferior and not worth mapping.[7]

One of the greatest deceptions of leaderoholism revolves around the notion that we are to gather and make followers for *ourselves.* What could be more damning and damaging than this wrongheaded idea? But it flows with astounding vigor in church leadership circles. The idea is, of course, never presented as such and would be categorically denied by just about any evangelical leader. But a thoughtful reflection on what today's pastors and church staffs have actually been absorbing into their thinking says otherwise.

Especially over the last decade or so, the evangelical world has been flooded with books, conferences, and seminars on leadership. Among the concepts being promoted are those that emphasize the importance of being a successful leader in order to attract successful leaders. This emphasis feeds and perpetuates the idea that we are called to build *great* organizations and to do this we have to be incredibly skilled and exceptional leaders ourselves because we are going to attract people like ourselves. Again, that sounds really good on the surface. But do you see the focus behind this concept? It makes everything revolve around *us*. Not *him*. Not Jesus.

It would be crazy for me to propose that we are not to do whatever it takes on our part to be the best at what we are called to do. I am not advocating that at all. Neither am I opposing excellence in ministry. At issue here is the idea that our aim as pastors and leaders should be to get people to follow *us* and ultimately to get *great* people to follow the greatness they see in us. Such an idea should be clearly understood as insidious. It is a mind-set that makes who *I* am the major interest. The concept is that *I* need to develop a magnetic skill set to such a degree that people will follow me so that ultimately I develop a great church.

Another idea influencing the evangelical world tells leaders that getting people to accept them as leaders is the prerequisite for getting people to accept their vision. This sounds innocuous enough. But let's take a moment and think it through. We are to sell ourselves *first* and then we will get to the Jesus stuff? So what would happen if we just give people Jesus straightaway? What if we give people Jesus and his vision? At issue is Jesus. When do we get to him?

When we lead with ourselves, we have left the trail of following Jesus. When we promote ourselves, we are diminishing the promotion of Jesus. John the Baptist, an incredibly charismatic individual with an innate ability to draw disciples to himself, knew he had to diminish the focus on himself in order to shine the spotlight on Jesus. He told his disciples, "The one who has the bride is the bridegroom. The friend of the bridegroom, who stands and hears him, rejoices greatly at the bridegroom's voice.

Therefore this joy of mine is now complete. He must increase, but I must decrease" (John 3:29-30).

Recently two longtime friends posted some wedding pictures online. I remembered the day, almost thirty years ago. There was Kim and Jerry, the bride and groom, along with the rest of the wedding party. I was one of the groomsmen, having grown up with them both. I looked through the pictures and reminisced about being with them that day. I also was reminded of what great hair I had then and how slim and trim I was. I think I looked pretty good. About fifty comments were posted by mutual friends after Kim and Jerry posted their wedding pictures. People commented about how great the couple looked—what a beautiful bride Kim was and how handsome a groom Jerry was. But do you know what? There was not one single comment about how good *I* looked. Not a mention of *me*. Why? The other three groomsmen and I were there to make this the best day of Jerry's life. We were there to support him and make the day about meeting his needs and wants. We were in the wedding to help shine the light on the bridegroom. To bring attention to ourselves at the wedding would have been totally out of place.

Jesus, the one and only, is *the* Leader with *the* vision. The rest of us—even the best of us—are called to point away from ourselves and clearly to *him*. To make Jesus the one and only premier focus must be our one and only premier focus. Just like a groomsman, we are honored to stand with the groom, but we are to fade into the crowd. Those in the wedding party are not there to see us. The spotlight is to be on the groom, on Jesus. Just as it was with John the Baptist, our joy will never be complete as long as we continue to increase the spotlight on ourselves at the expense of shining it on Jesus.

Again, the idea perpetuated by the contemporary church's leadership obsession, that we are tasked with getting others to follow *us*, pushes Jesus into the shadows. The stake I want to drive into the ground here is that we need to become better followers and servants of Jesus, who point to him. To focus on getting people to buy into us is beyond a slippery slope. It is a vertical drop.

A further concept given much attention in evangelical circles is the idea that leadership is all about having the skill set to acquire followers. The million-dollar question that should be asked is, "Followers of whom?" The near wholesale buy-in of this starting point within the leadership rhetoric of the contemporary church is rampant. It has become the foundation of Leadership 101. The lesson is that people have to go through our leadership greatness before they can get to Jesus.

The subtlety here lies in the twisted ideology that we should be setting about the task of getting people to follow *us*. Now many readers may say, "Of course that is not the intention. That is understood." I agree that that is not the intention, but I disagree that this is understood. My experience with pastors and church leaders makes it abundantly clear that most of them believe they must be super leaders to get people to follow them, and getting people to follow them should always be squarely in mind. This necessitates an almost ceaseless self-centered focus. Not only does this ideology constantly train a person's eyes and heart away from Jesus, but also it loads on that person tremendous pressure and stress as he or she strives for leadership greatness. For a pastor or ministry staff member to fail at "leadership" is considered near to ultimate failure.

SOBERING UP

I considered beginning this chapter with, "Hi, my name is Lance. I'm a leaderoholic." This is very familiar territory for me. If I am qualified to write on this subject, it is only because I am a recovering leaderoholic myself. After years and years of drinking from the leadership tap and striving to create the best "Leader Lance" possible, I finally hit the wall. I wasn't sure if I had reached the proverbial point of burnout, was in a midlife crisis, or had just gotten bored of pastoring. The only thing I was certain of was that I could not continue on in the way I was going.

I attended all the high-voltage leadership conferences and spent enormous amounts of time and money on leadership books. My own "leadership capacity" was a constant matter of attention for me. A close second was the development of "more and better" leaders in the church where I was the "lead" pastor. My leadership was trumping Jesus' lordship in my actual daily focus and pursuit. For me, the obsessive self-focus became evident one day when I read a passage I had read literally thousands of times before. This time it finally hit home. This time it read *me*. "Come to me, all who labor and are heavy laden, and I will give you rest. Take my yoke upon you, and learn from me, for I am gentle and lowly in heart, and you will find rest for your souls. For my yoke is easy, and my burden is light" (Matt. 11:28-30).

This passage might as well have been from a Jules Verne novel. "Wow, that would be a great place to live," I thought, "but I can't relate to that at all. Leading this church is anything but 'easy,' and the burden I feel is anything but 'light.' And I certainly do not feel 'rest' in my soul. I'm stressed out most of the time." I sat for about an hour, just staring, moving my eyes back and forth from this passage to the wooded area outside my office window. I began to have a long conversation with myself, "If Jesus was not lying—and if his 'yoke is [truly] easy' and his 'burden is [truly] light'—then there is only one conclusion: I must be wearing someone else's yoke, and I must be carrying someone else's burden." "Where is this constant pressure coming from?" I wondered.

This was the point in my journey where I realized that much of the stress I felt, as a lead pastor, was self-inflicted. I was living life in a perpetual *leaderohol* stupor. I was binging on leadership and suffering constant leadership hangovers. My head hurt from all the strategic thinking, initiative scheming, and organizational guruizing I had become convinced was necessary for steering a "successful" church. Jesus was pretty much nonexistent in most of it. My soul was pickled and parched at the same time. I was thirsting for the presence of the very

Christ who had been crowded out of my soul by the obsession of leading *for* him.

I began to look at my job description—not the one filed away on my computer or in a desk drawer—my mental job description. I started to think through all the things *I* was supposed to be as the "lead" pastor. Here is what I came up with:

- An expert theologian
- An expert communicator
- An expert visionary
- An expert on marriage
- An expert on sex
- An expert on parenting
- An expert administrator
- An expert manager
- An expert CEO
- The face of the church

That's all. Sure. No problem.

Fitting Jesus into my schedule had become a chore in itself. I had to admit that I was too distracted by *leading* for him to keep my eyes on *following* him. After all, the church experts were telling me I had to be a great leader because I first had to get people to follow *me*. It was just assumed that I would be following Christ as I led for him.

Herein lies another issue—the assumption that most leaders are following Christ in the first place. To follow Jesus goes way beyond saluting the Four Spiritual Laws and having a consistent quiet time. It means to walk in his footsteps. It means to pattern one's life after what Jesus said and did. To follow Jesus means to follow him in the way he treated people, regardless of their social status or what they could give him in return. It means to follow his gentleness, humility, kindness, and love in the most strident of circumstances. Following Jesus means treating the people that you work with on a daily basis with goodness and brotherly love.

As we move through part I of this book, we will look at how the leadership obsession so often draws us off the path of followership and away from the posture of a servant. How did we get to this place? Over four decades of marinating in church growth theory has left the vast majority of evangelical denominational and local church leaders wandering in the weeds of a consumer church field. It has created a clergy crop that views the church from the perspective of marketers and businesspersons and a Christian mass that views itself as clientele.

A lot of finger pointing has emerged as leaders decry Christians who are consumers of religious goods and services. But what should we have expected? We (leaders) are the ones that created the church consumer culture in the first place. Christians in North America have become who we made them to be. Our obsession with the corporate marketing tactics approach to leading the church feeds the obsession for Christians to look for the "best deal" on a church. Neil Cole comments on this phenomenon: "Many pastors complain about the consumeristic mind-set in their churches. It is a 'what-have-you-done-for-me-lately' attitude that causes the pastor to feel pressure to keep up with the megachurch around the corner. But our people have a consumeristic attitude because we have trained them to think this way. When we try to 'sell' our worship and programs to the largest crowd possible, we will attract and reinforce a consumer mind-set."[8]

IS LEADERSHIP NECESSARY?

No one needs to convince me that today's church needs leadership. It needs it as much as ever. By no means am I saying there should be no leadership in the church. That is not my beef and not the message of this book. The most pressing issue, or question, is what *kind* of leadership should exist in the church? What does leadership in the church mean? Or what *should* it mean? My chief concern is tied to the most common patterns of leadership we see in the church—how leadership has been twisted and distorted in the way it is defined, modeled, and practiced.

Second, leadership has become the dominant focus for those who have been called by God into roles as guides and servants for the body of Christ. It has literally become an obsession. I have heard Leonard Sweet call it the "leadership fetish." It has become an industry unto itself within the church world. All the while, discipleship has languished.

A recent report based on a joint research project conducted between the Exponential Church Planting Network and LifeWay Christian Resources highlights the concern. In the report, titled *7 Top Issues Church Planters Face*, Ed Stetzer explained that the research was based on interviews with over thirty well-known leaders who had over six hundred years of cumulative experience working with hundreds of church planters. Stetzer then began to unpack the findings:

> Leadership development is the most frequently cited challenge of planters according to our research in this survey of church planting leaders and thinkers. Leadership issues included recruiting and developing leaders; implementing teams; creating a reproducible leadership development approach; developing a leader/oversight/elder board; hiring and leading staff; discerning changes required to facilitate growth; healthy decision making; and delegating and empowering volunteers.[9]

In a subsequent post, Stetzer continued:

> I asked [Darrin Patrick], "Why do most churches stay small?" Darrin explained:

> > Largely because most pastors don't know how to build systems, structures, and processes that are not contingent upon them. Most pastors can care for people, but don't build systems of care. Most pastors can develop leaders individually, but lack the skill to implement a process of leadership development. When a pastor can't build systems and structures that support ministry, the only people who are cared for or empowered to lead are those who are "near" the pastor or those very close to

the pastor. This limits the size of the church to the size of the pastor.[10]

Todd Wilson, who leads the Exponential network, also commented on the report:

> Discipleship is cited as a uniquely . . . separate thing from leadership development in the report. Where leadership development is in the context of building the institution bigger, discipleship is in the context of growing the believer better. . . . What if our paradigm of seeing them as distinct . . . is actually part of the problem? Isn't it strange that we are coming off two to three decades of LEADERSHIP . . . as the silver bullet (or pill) for everything and now . . . we've entered a period where the most elusive, frustrating issue for most pastors is with ineffectiveness in DISCIPLESHIP? Down deep most know . . . we are struggling to make disciples who are a distinctly different aroma to the world.[11]

I believe Wilson's conclusions are right on. Discipleship has suffered in obscurity. It's been choked out by leadership smoke. The wood needed to keep the fires of discipleship and followership burning has been hijacked to the furnaces of leadership development. Is it really true that the most pressing need in our churches has to do with the complexity of systems, structures, and processes? Or does the *real* need have to do with abandoning our addiction to artificial, institutionalized leadership forms and returning to the task of disciple making by following Jesus?

It is as if we have built restaurants when we should have built culinary schools. We have spent most of our resources and time on feeding people rather than training them to feed themselves and others. If understanding systems and structures of organizational wizardry is so vital to the expansion and operation of the church, why didn't the writers of the New Testament provide guidance on the subject? The fact we feel we must look beyond the Scriptures to gain an understanding of this subject should be a strong hint that God is not interested in it in the first place.

In the movie *The Shawshank Redemption*, Red, played by Morgan Freeman, reflects on the news that Brooks, a recently paroled lifelong prisoner, had hung himself: "These walls are funny. First you hate 'em, then you get used to 'em. Enough time passes, you get so you depend on them. That's institutionalized."[12]

Prisoners become institutionalized because they have lost the ability to make decisions on their own. The controllers above them make the key decisions. They tell the prisoners when to wake up, when to eat, when to shower, when to exercise, and when to sleep. Could it be that our need for the current systems and processes of care exist because we fail to make disciples in the first place? Could it be that the "follow me" path, laid down by Jesus, is intended to be the system itself?

The near wholesale abandonment of the "follow me" message and pattern has left us with institutionalized Christians by the millions. While most pastors are consumed with getting people to follow them to *do church*, very few pastors can point to a handful of individuals they have invited to follow them as they *do life*. Most Christians have scant ability to mine the rich fields of Scripture for themselves. The Christian living sections at bookstores get bigger and bigger as Christians try to figure out this "complicated" lifestyle that the early church simply called "the Way" (see Acts 9:2).

This is the primary reason for the need of the weekly motivational talk that we call the sermon. Many of the believers in our churches are in utter dependence on the weekly sermon because they were never trained to study the Bible for themselves. And I dare say that many pastors are unknowingly addicted to the adrenalin that comes from mesmerizing an audience each week. I am convinced that much of this is undiagnosed codependency. I have conversed with many ministers not currently pastoring a church who talk about how much they miss preaching on a regular basis, but I cannot recall one conversation where one of them has said they miss mentoring (discipling) others.

Jesus had to "unteach" his first followers quite a bit. Their entire understanding of the coming of the kingdom of God meant power and domination. Few of us today are any different. Discipleship to Jesus means we must be as quick and willing to unlearn as we are to learn—probably more so. It seems that no sooner had Jesus' disciples settled into the rhythm of following him than they had developed personal ambitions to capitalize on their position as his companions. Similar ambitions exist across the evangelical Christian landscape today.

There are several instances in which we observe Jesus' first followers asking the wrong questions. They were consumed with thoughts concerning their own positions and leadership status. The brothers James and John come to mind. James and John wanted to ensure their rank in what they assumed would be a hierarchical government, established by Jesus. They wanted it so bad that they got their mother to talk to Jesus about letting them have the top spots in his administration—which they were sure he was going to establish (see Matt. 20:20-21).

Look around and you will see that little has changed today. In the camps of Christianity we have placed a disproportionate focus on subjects and issues orbiting around leadership. At the time of this writing a quick search of books on the subjects of Christian leadership and discipleship at Amazon.com brought up about twenty-four thousand books. Of these books, 35 percent were on discipleship and 65 percent were on Christian leadership. Only 2 percent of the books mentioned followership, and the overwhelming majority of those were not related to the subject of Christianity. This does not take into account the massive amount of non-Christian leadership books that are read by pastors and church planters.

If we compare these ratios to New Testament verses that mention "discipleship," "following," and "leadership," the results are stunning. The word "disciple" is mentioned 260 times, the phrase "follow me" is used 23 times, and the word "lead" or "leader" is mentioned only 7 times. That is a forty to one ratio of discipleship/followership to leadership.

Granted, the metrics above are simply an unscientific stab at gaining an understanding of what the Christian leadership community has its eyes trained on. I do not present it as empirical data, but it is telling at the very least. When will Jesus' emphasis become our emphasis? When will we *hear* what Jesus was saying in response to James and John's fixation on leadership?

TWO

BUSINESS AS USUAL
FROM GOD TO GREAT

Unless the LORD builds the house, those who build it labor in vain.

—Ps. 127:1

I am absolutely convinced that 100 years from now, many books will be written on the phenomenon that is the late 20th Century/early 21st Century American church. And I am fairly certain . . . that people, in reading about it, will say to each other: "You must be joking! Seriously???! People actually thought it was a good idea to structure the Church as if it were a business? Honestly?!"

—Mike Breen[1]

everal years ago the church I planted and pastored was in the midst of a building project. Believing that we could save money, we chose to do some of the labor ourselves. We had several weekend-warrior carpenters. A lot of us watched HGTV and *This Old House* on television and we figured we were up to the task. There was actually only one genuine professional among us. Notwithstanding, we were a crew that was dangerously confident enough to go for it.

After a few weeks of framing walls everything had gone fairly smooth and the time had arrived to hang drywall. This was a milestone we had eagerly looked forward to. When drywall goes up, rooms and spaces get defined and a building project starts to look as though something is really happening. About eight of us gathered on a nice spring evening, eager and ready to take the project to the next level. After a fifteen-minute quick course by Harper, our resident pro, we commenced the project. We began working in a large room with very high ceilings, pairing off in the corners of the room. This meant that four teams were able to work the room all at once. Harper would oversee the operation and troubleshoot along the way. As the work got under way, the room was filled with testosterone and confident machismo.

It didn't take long before we needed Harper's troubleshooting. After hanging just a few sheets of drywall, each team began to mention that the drywall was not meeting the studs at the proper places. If studs are installed properly, drywall sheets will lay halfway across the edge of each stud, leaving space for the next sheet to fit and be screwed to the stud. But this wasn't happening. The sheets were hanging past the studs in some places and short of the studs in other places. Guys had to reposition studs throughout the room almost every time they began to lay a sheet of drywall. The only saving grace was that they had used metal studs that could be unscrewed and repositioned fairly easily. But to say the least, progress was slow and frustrating.

What had begun as an optimistic and energetic night quickly turned into a defeated bunch of wannabe Bob Vilas, dumbfounded and complaining. After about an hour of this fiasco, Harper shouted for everyone to stop. It is important at this point for the reader to have a clear picture of Harper. He is a rough-hewn Midwesterner who looks and acts like Paul Sr. of *American Chopper* fame, down to the signature Fu Manchu mustache.

Harper yelled, "You Nancies, get over here!" Pulling out his tape measure and hanging it on the cross section of a sawhorse, he stretched it out several feet. With his signature gravelly voice, he grumbled, "Some of you guys throw your tape measures out alongside of mine." Four or five guys obliged, stretching their tape measures parallel to Harper's. "Read 'em," he said. "What do you see?"

At first glance none of us had a clue of what it was we were supposed to be seeing. It seemed simple enough. There were five tape measures lying next to each other. "What are we missing here?" I wondered. "What is Harper pulling on us?" "Get in there and look closer," Harper snarled. "Oh no!" one of the guys said. "Look at that. The measurements are different." Sure enough, they were. We had five tape measures and at least three differing measurements. The tape measures did not all match up. The first few feet the measurements looked the same, but when we looked several feet down the line, the disparity began to appear.

Along with the rest of our crew, I had always assumed that a tape measure is a tape measure is a tape measure. An inch is an inch, and a foot is a foot. It had never dawned on any of us that all tape measures are not alike. Harper picked up a scrap of drywall and wrote the brand name and model number of his own tape measure on it and sent one of our guys, Dan, to the hardware store to buy a dozen tape measures. He told the rest of us to take a coffee break until Dan returned.

When the tape measures arrived, Harper instituted a statute that was to be in place for the remainder of our building project. Those tape measures would be the one and only model allowed on the job site. They were placed on a shelf, and from that point on anyone working on the project was instructed to grab one as soon as he arrived and to return it when he left. Drywall installation would have to wait. We spent the next week repositioning studs.

Looking back on this situation I find it ironic that we learned this lesson while actually constructing a church building. Metaphorically this is precisely what has happened over several decades and continues with full steam in the church today. God says, "Here is how I want you to build. Here are your blueprints and metrics. Use these." But we have better ideas. Better ways—our own ways—and means of leading.

IN OUR OWN IMAGE

You shall have no other gods before me. You shall not make for yourself a carved image, or any likeness of anything that is in heaven above, or that is in the earth beneath, or that is in the water under the earth. (Exod. 20:3-4)

Rousseau is widely credited with saying, "God created man in his own image. And man returned the favor." The second statute of the Ten Commandments forbids us from creating images depicting the elements of the heavenly realm. Why so? Because the standards of the kingdom of God are unique. Of the many reasons for this prohibition we must admit that not only do our artificial images always fall short of the glorious standard of God himself, but they eventually replace God in our minds as well. Our images, mental or physical, begin to shape our concepts of who God is and what he is concerned with. In short, they become our idols. And we, the idol makers, ultimately receive the lion's share of the glory and adulation.

The Lord is determined to etch our images of his character—who he is and how he is—into this world without our help. We must admit that we break this commandment in a myriad of ways. We overlay our own ideas and attitudes on most everything we *think* God thinks. Each of us is convinced that God sees things as we see them.

My friend Neil Cole says,

Our church ministries have become high-profile organizations built on a business model. We have strong dynamic leaders at the top who are responsible to set the culture and direction of the ministry. The weight of the organization is placed on the leader, and unfortunately, little is placed on Jesus. In our eyes, a strong leader can make or break a church, and Jesus has little to do with it, except to bring us a real Savior—a dynamic preacher/leader/CEO.[2]

We have done exactly what the Israelites did thousands of years ago:

All the elders of Israel got together and confronted Samuel at Ramah. They presented their case: "Look, you're an old man, and your sons aren't following in your footsteps. Here's what we want you to do: Appoint a king to rule us, just like everybody else." . . . .

God answered Samuel, "Go ahead and do what they're asking. They are not rejecting you. They've rejected me as their King. From the day I brought them out of Egypt until this very day they've been behaving like this, leaving me for other gods. And now they're doing it to you. So let them have their own way. But warn them of what they're in for. Tell them the way kings operate, just what they're likely to get from a king." (1 Sam. 8:4-5, 7-9, TM)

The people of Israel demanded a king, "just like everybody else," although God wanted to be their King. The church has done the same thing in its leadership fixation. Countless times I have heard pastors say, "The church is a business" or "You have to run the church like a business." Evangelical leaders have ingested this idea across the West. And it is an insidious mistake.

It is time we dumb down leadership and smarten up followership. The combination of viewing the church through Newtonian mechanized thinking, as if it were a machine, with the human default toward dominating others, has created a convoluted perspective of leading and managing. Co-following in the kingdom of the new King turns most of our understanding and experience of organizations and people management inside out and upside down. There is a better way.

And Jesus called them to him and said to them, "You know that those who are considered rulers of the Gentiles lord it over them, and their great ones exercise authority over them. But it shall not be so among you. But whoever would be great among you must be your servant." (Mark 10:42-43)

It will "not be so among you." The new King of the new kingdom declares a new way—his way. King Jesus says, "You are not going to use authority in the way the rest of the world uses it. You will not dominate one another the way the kingdoms of this age do." He then points out two distinguishing factors between followers in his kingdom and the leaders in kingdoms of the world:

- They (worldly leaders) "lord" it over others. The phrase used here means "to subject to oneself, to subdue, to master."
- They (worldly leaders) "exercise authority" over others. This phrase means "to wield power" over another.

When we become beholden to earthly ways of leading and managing, we become part of the very system Jesus came to destroy. And along the way we fail to develop disciples, which is the task he gave us. We exchange the basin and towel of a servant for the scepter and crown of a king. We cling to the kingdoms of this world and fail to enter the kingdom of God and to become and multiply followers of Jesus. Fleshly ways never produce spiritual fruit.

I have been involved in church planting for almost twenty years. Part of the process of developing new church planters begins with assessing men and women on their potential for success. I have yet to find an acceptable turnkey church planter assessment tool that emphasizes the followership and servantship of Jesus—his persona, character, and ways of developing disciples. The majority of current assessment processes are fixated on management concerns, preaching skill, strategic administrative acumen, and such. They are focused on leadership at the expense of followership and servantship.

One of today's most prominent groups that is self-described as a church-planting network uses a grading system that labels candidates (men only are eligible, by the way) as "A guys" or "B guys." They will only support the "A guys," men who they are convinced can grow a large church. I see no possible way that Jesus' original twelve recruits would garner the A grade from this group's assessment. Sometimes I wonder if the only guy from Jesus' crew of disciples that would have been certified as "qualified" by most church-planting groups would have been Judas, the treasurer.

I am friends with a team of church planters in Colorado Springs that is guided by two young men who failed the assessment used by their denomination. One of the guys actually had to attend professional therapy because he was so shaken by the assessment team that told him he was not church planter material because he lacked "leadership" skills on several levels. Thankfully wiser minds prevailed and talked both guys "off the ledge," and the two young men made the move from California to begin the work in Colorado. A year later a plethora of life-changing stories are surfacing as a vibrant missional community of servant-disciples of Jesus has flourished through the guidance of these two "B guys."

WHEN JESUS HATES

It is difficult to place the word "hate" next to Jesus. It stuns the senses. We just don't think of hate and Jesus ever going together, especially when we think of Jesus as the one doing the hating. But a New Testament passage tells us there is indeed something Jesus hates. You would think that when the Bible says Jesus *hates* anything, we would stand up and take note. In Rev. 2:6 Jesus tells the church in Ephesus, "You hate the works of the Nicolaitans, which I also hate." Just a few verses later (v.

15) the Nicolaitans are mentioned again: "You have some who hold the teaching of the Nicolaitans."

The root of the word "nicolaitan" comes from the Greek words *nikos*, which means "victory" or "conquest," and *laos*, which means "people." We get the word "laity" from *laos*. The compound of these Greek words means "conquest over the people" and points to the earliest forms of a priestly or clergy class in the church.[3] Church history shows us that a full-blown clerical system developed relatively quickly in the early life of the church. By the mid-sixteenth century the Council of Trent announced, "If anyone shall say that there is not in the Catholic Church a hierarchy established by the divine ordination, consisting of bishops, presbyters and ministers, let him be anathema."[4]

How amazing is that? This declaration directly contradicts several clear statements Jesus and the apostles made in reference to hierarchy. The issue of ministry gifting and guidance by gifted individuals is not in question. The problem is the hierarchy and the dominating, conquering ways and means behind the structures it creates, coupled with the behavior of those who maintain them. The insidious nature of Nicolaitanism lies in the separation between normal saints and elevated leaders. Take note, Jesus doesn't merely *dislike* this stuff. He doesn't *prefer* things were not this way. He categorically *hates* it!

When leaders lose their "follower" self-view, dichotomies and hierarchical positioning manifests. As soon as a person defines himself or herself by his or her ranking in the community of saints, that person has gone off the rails of following Christ. No matter the role you occupy in your church or faith community, your primary identity should be as a follower and servant of Jesus. I agree with my former seminary professor Eddie Gibbs, who says, "The controlling style of leadership that is so prevalent among the builder and boomer generations, and that typically determines the church's corporate culture, must give way to this empowering, connective style if the church is to reinvent itself to meet the missional challenges and opportunities of a new day."[5]

Regardless of the clear commandments concerning the issue, the ink was not even dry in the New Testament before people began ignoring Jesus' words. The apostle John challenged one individual, calling him out by name, for his ambitious desire to stand above the believers in the local church: "I have written something to the church, but Diotrephes, *who likes to put himself first*, does not acknowledge our authority" (3 John v. 9, emphasis added).

Diotrephes, very likely, was a gifted follower. The problem was that he loved preeminence and wanted to be *first*. He viewed himself as top dog and wanted everyone else to see him that way as well. I can't help but wonder if he called himself senior rabbi, lead herder, or maybe executive shepherd. This verse takes on even more impact when you consider that many churches today are structured with one guy on top. They claim to have plurality of leadership with a *first* among equals—the very language used in this verse.

FORBIDDEN TITLES

None of us would want Jesus to lump him or her into the same category as that of the scribes and Pharisees. This is precisely what he did with those who want titles of esteem and notoriety attached to their names.

And they love the place of honor at feasts and the best seats in the synagogues and greetings in the marketplaces and being called rabbi by others. But you are not to be called rabbi, for you have one teacher, and you are all brothers. And call no man your father on earth, for you have one Father, who is in heaven. Neither be called instructors, for you have one instructor, the Christ. The greatest among you shall be your servant. Whoever exalts himself will be humbled, and whoever humbles himself will be exalted. (Matt. 23:6-12)

If you are a parent, you probably know what it is like to have your child ignore your explicit instructions. You told him or her not to do something, or to do something, only to discover he or she did the opposite. You then say, "Do you think I was talking just to hear myself? Did you hear *anything* I told you?" Well, Jesus must be saying that right now because he could not have been clearer. He said, "No titles." The titles are reserved for him and God alone. Jesus said, "You have *one* teacher, *one* Father, and *one* instructor." And he pointed out, "You all are brothers." He flattened the hierarchical ideals. Splat! Jesus said we are all brothers. We are not a corporation. We are a family. Jesus said, "If you want to be great, become a servant."

Jesus was emphatic. He forbade titles. He permitted no place for them. Why so, we may wonder. For one thing, titles are meant to create categories and separators. They highlight status, for better or worse. Titles always position one person or group over the other and create boundaries, fences, and doors that need permission or privilege for entry. Titles change the entire dynamic of a relationship, creating a new set of rules and limits of expression, openness, and authenticity. As soon as a title is applied to one person, the title "less than or greater than" is pinned to the other. Titles create psychological and sociological dynamics of hierarchy.

For example, imagine that you enter into a conversation with a stranger at a party, conference, or social gathering. A mutual friend approaches and says to you that Gary (the stranger) is the president of Acme Oil or the owner of Triple A Logistics. Then Gary asks, "So what do *you* do?" At this moment the relationship changes. You and Gary are now distinguished and categorized—and you both are very much aware of it.

I have a buddy that told me about his friend who was a youth pastor at a large church in Dallas. The church is led by a prominent pastor who is regularly featured on television and radio. One day as they passed one another in a hallway, the young man greeted the pastor with, "Hi, Jim."[6] The famed minister stopped, walked over to the youth pastor, and—locking eyes with him—slowly said, "It's Dr. Smith." On another occasion I listened in amazement to a sermon by a gigachurch pastor from Tulsa who impassionedly shared an account of one of his church members seeing him in a local shopping mall and calling out, "Hey, Willy!" He was deeply offended and related this incident in his sermon to his congregation. He instructed his church that calling him by his first name, rather than the title "pastor" was dishonoring and anathema.

Someone may point out that Paul opened some of his epistles with his title "apostle." I would argue that the reference to his apostleship was not in any sense an emphasis of it as a *title* but of his *role* in relation to his God-given calling. Nevertheless, in the majority of his letters, Paul opened by calling himself a "slave of Jesus." This is the same Paul who instructed us to shun status and privilege:

> Think of yourselves the way Christ Jesus thought of himself. He had equal status with God but didn't think so much of himself that he had to cling to the advantages of that status no matter what. Not at all. When the time came, he set aside the privileges of deity and took on the status of a slave, became human! Having become human, he stayed human. It was an incredibly humbling process. He didn't claim special privileges. Instead, he lived a selfless, obedient life and then died a selfless, obedient death—and the worst kind of death at that—a crucifixion. (Phil. 2:5-7, TM)

Paul says Jesus set aside his privileges, took on the status of a slave, and lived a selfless life. If we stake the claim that we are followers of Jesus, it means we follow his pattern. We follow his way—*the Way*. Any form of leadership that clings to privilege, eschews the posture of a slave, and lives selfishly is denying the true Christ. Churches with leadership cultures fueled by a privilege-taking few are being led by people who are not following Christ from the very epicenter of who he is.

THE CORRUPTION OF POWER

It is probably not an overstatement to say that the most common styles, methods, and forms of leadership that dominate the church today have been molded in humanity's own image. This is certainly true of our schematics of power and authority. Alan and Debra Hirsch reflect on this issue:

The fallen desire for power over others profoundly distorts our understanding of Christian faith, and with it the revelation of God received in the incarnation of Jesus.

. . . In a situation where power is being abused, the leader will grow only to the height to which the crowd raises him, but he or she ends up in the same state of servitude as the crowd—they are transformed by the very power they exercise. . . . Rather than freeing people by helping them relate to Jesus as Lord, control freaks, true to the tendency of the narcissistic personality, actually feed on the needs and adulation of those they lead.[7]

It is clear that Jesus' first disciples were convinced of a future hierarchy in the kingdom of God. They also wanted, and expected, positions of honor and rank in Jesus' administration. Two thousand years later, many of Jesus' followers are obsessed with the wrong questions and pursuits. The scary thing is that most conferences on church leadership and church planting (including most church-planting systems) involve similar ideas.

We see the nonrelational nature of hierarchical power highlighted by the words of VISA founder Dee Hock:

One who is coerced to the purposes, objectives, or preferences of another is not a follower in any true sense of the word, but an object of manipulation. Nor is the relationship materially altered if both parties voluntarily accept the dominance of one by the other. A true leader cannot be bound to lead. A true follower cannot be bound to follow. The moment they are bound they are no longer leader or follower. If the behavior of either is compelled, whether by force, economic necessity, or contractual arrangement, the relationship is altered to one of superior/subordinate, manager/employee, master/servant, or owner/slave.[8]

What is Jesus' answer to this? It is emphatic: "But it shall not be so among you" (Mark 10:43). My hunch is that when Jesus spoke this sentence, he said it something like this: "But [pause for effect] it shall *not* [pause for effect] be so [with pointed finger] among *you!*"

Jesus tells his tribe of first followers, "For your entire lives you have watched people dominate and control one another based on caste, charisma, stature, status, rank, and position. But *my* kingdom doesn't work that way. It will not work that way. In fact, I forbid you to try to make it work that way! The *greatest* among you will be the servant among you."

Seminary professor Rusty Ricketson has written an excellent book, *Follower First*, in which he emphasizes the need for leaders to be followers (first). On the idea that our churches are to be communities of equal co-followers (though some individuals serve in the capacity of guides performing the tasks of leading) with Jesus viewed as the only capital *L* Leader in our churches, Ricketson writes,

> Biblical follower activity is based upon the freedom the followers have to exercise their gifts, talents and abilities. This level of follower activity is based upon two aspects. First, a follower's level of intimacy with the Leader, the Lord Jesus Christ, determines the level and activity of following within the context of the church. Followers who have a keen desire to know Christ in all aspects of life are usually actively engaged in the process of making Christ known resulting in these followers having a greater degree of responsibility and influence in the church and among the leaders. Second, the titular leaders of the church must establish a permission giving atmosphere in which the follower is secure to initiate activity without fear of reprisal. Leaders do not empower followers. Rather leaders create the structural freedom in which followers can exercise their gifts and abilities. Such freedom results in high follower participation and greater productivity.

The interdependent nature and the humility required of persons within the biblical follower-leader relationship allow both followers and leaders the freedom to serve within the scope of their giftedness. In a follower-centric organization, position and rank are not highly prized. Therefore, followers and leaders can cooperate with each other under the lordship of Christ without fear of being replaced or being upstaged by someone else.[9]

There is a stark contrast in posture and demeanor here. Again, we need humans to carry out the *task* of leading, but our identity and posture must never be as a capital *L* Leader. I hope you see the difference between the two. The push back against power structures, which are underwritten with titles that remind everyone continually of the proper rank and file, is to fashion hearts and a community of Christ's servants. We find Dee Hock helpful again:

> In the deepest sense, distinction between leaders and followers is meaningless. In every moment of life, we are simultaneously leading and following. There is never a time when our knowledge, judgment and wisdom are not more useful and applicable than that of another. There is never a time when the knowledge, judgment and wisdom of another are not more useful and applicable than ours. At any time that "other" may be superior, subordinate, or peer.[10]

In the kingdom of God we must view Jesus as our big *L* Leader—the one and only Senior Shepherd. Men and women can, and should, *function* in leadership but never be underscored with rank as leaders. Leadership must be viewed as a spiritual gift and not as a position of power. To develop the familial culture of a Jesus community requires us to jettison any hint of corporate-style, top-down authority structure, along with the language that supports it.

One former church staff member shared his experience of joining the staff of a leadership-centric church:

> "Something just changed," I said to myself as I closed the door. After ten years as the senior pastor of a midsize church I had planted in the northwest suburbs of a Midwest city, I was now a "staff pastor" at a Southern megachurch. About fifteen minutes into unpacking boxes as I moved into my new office, the senior pastor popped in to see how I was coming along and to "shoot a couple things" my way. He had been a part of my life for several years as a friend,

mentor, and unofficial coach. I had always been comfortable around him and felt treated as a respected partner in the kingdom of God and . . . in all the church stuff we both were involved in. But these last five or so minutes were different. I wasn't exactly sure how to articulate it, but something felt very unusual about the atmosphere. It was hard for me to put my finger on it. I was certain about one thing, though. Our relationship had just changed. Stepping into a church leadership system structured on hierarchy meant that I was only a peer with the "lead guy" on a limited basis. I soon discovered that I couldn't work *with* him, only *for* him.[11]

CULTURES OF DOMINANCE

Within the culture of the corporate business world are leadership patterns of forcible command and control. These structures include protocols of who can and cannot be questioned, consulted, or criticized. Overtones of fear are sprinkled throughout such companies. Employees learn quickly when and when not to speak, and to never speak up. If you make the mistake of doing so, you could soon be gone—in the twinkling of an eye.

I recently shared dinner with a young man who had just recently been fired from a church he had served for several years. He made the mistake of sending an email to the upper echelon—the executive leadership team—that questioned the decision of following through with a costly building program for a wedding chapel during a season of staffing cutbacks. He merely requested a dialogue among the entire staff to get a consensus of thought on the situation. His email was written in a very respectful and humble manner. The day after Devon[12] sent the email two members of the executive leadership team showed up at his office to inform him that he was being let go, effective immediately. The reason he was given for being fired was that he had "incited negative morale and displayed a lack of cooperation." When Devon asked why he had not been given the opportunity to at least discuss the situation, per Jesus' Matt. 18

instructions on dealing with conflict, one of the two "execs" told him he shouldn't be surprised. "If this was Sprint, or another business, it would be done just like this," she replied.

What is the problem with this scenario? It is that the church *is not* Sprint, nor any other business. The church is the body of Christ, and it has a manual of protocol. It's called the Bible. And if these "leaders" were following Jesus, they would never consider such behavior or tactics. The thing that should terrify us is that this type of scenario is a commonly accepted practice across the landscape of evangelical churches and denominations.

Organizational charts and job descriptions serve as visual reminders of the pecking order in the corporate business world. And most of today's evangelical churches, especially the larger ones, have similar documents. But we find them in smaller churches as well. I recently came across a sixty-member church whose website profiled the "senior" pastor and the "executive" pastor. If it were not such a seriously sad issue, it would be laughable. The leadership obsession is rampant.

People who are motivated by the ways of the world can see no way other than command and control as a means for orderliness. But order and control do not have to go hand in hand. Management professor Margaret Wheatley remarks,

> If people are machines, seeking to control us makes sense. But if we live with the same forces intrinsic to all other life, then seeking to impose control though rigid structures is suicide. If we believe that there is no order to human activity except that imposed by the leader, that there is no self-regulation except that dictated by policies, if we believe that responsible leaders must have their hands into everything, controlling every decision, person, and moment, then we cannot hope for anything except what we already have—a treadmill of frantic efforts that end up destroying our individual and collective vitality.[13]

At the root of command-and-control structures is fear. And fear is the opposite of faith. When we find churches with leadership cultures of dominance, and the accompanying fear-engendering atmospheres they create, at their hearts are the controllers, who (with titles to signal their authority) are the ones who truly walk in fear. The fear they emit has its source in the fear gripping their own psyches. If you currently serve, or have served, on staff at a church like this, you know what I am speaking of here. The ugly monster of human power found no safe harbor in the early church. The apostle Paul said, "And I was with you in weakness and in fear and much trembling, and my speech and my message were not in plausible words of wisdom, but in demonstration of the Spirit and of power, so that your faith might not rest in the wisdom of men but in the power of God" (1 Cor. 2:3-5).

As an example for us to follow, Paul said it was the power of the Holy Spirit that he demonstrated and relied on. It was not the wisdom or leadership power of humans. Denver pastor Kathy Escobar says, "The main problem . . . is that we, as people and communities, are generally addicted to power. We are strangely drawn to it. We tend to want more of it ourselves or to surround ourselves with those who have it. We are far too eager to grant power to those who abuse it."[14]

THE NEWTONIAN EFFECT

Perhaps you know the routine. The room is filled with flip charts of lists, calendars, acronyms, assignments, plans, and projections. The strategizing session is aimed at leading the church to the next level. But the church is not a machine, and our approaches are a mismatch. The "church growth era" church has fallen into the trap of substituting the voice of the Lord for strategic initiatives. Newton and Descartes gave us the triumph of reason, and we have made it our chief approach to guiding the church. Charting our course through predictable planning has become a replacement for the Holy Spirit as our guide. The rational approach has replaced the biblical approach. We organize people into boxes according to their roles. They are treated as we would treat parts of machinery, and our organizational charts specify their responsibilities and functions, deciding where and how they fit and when and what they are allowed to speak.[15]

In the Newtonian age science sought to displace God. The current malady for the contemporary church is that by attempting to lead ministries by way of the science of predictable management methods, God is often shoved out. The Rev. 3:20 image of Jesus standing outside his own church, knocking to be let in, has never been timelier. He has effectively been pushed out of the strategic-planning meeting by accords and schematics that often contradict his very persona. Wheatley says, "At present, our most sophisticated way of acknowledging the world's complexity is to build elaborate system maps, which are most often influenced by a quest for predictability. When we create a map—displaying what we think are all the relevant elements and interactions—we hope to be able to manipulate the system for the outcomes we desire. We are thinking like good Newtonians."[16]

I have attended more strategic church staff meetings than I can count, where an obligatory ceremonial prayer is offered up before getting down to the business of figuring out the future of the particular local church or ministry. The quickest thinker in the room is soon standing at the whiteboard, marker in hand, charting and scoring the course for the next twelve months or so. The Holy Spirit was saluted from the outset (opening prayer) and will be saluted again after the planning session. But during the strategizing itself, it will be skill sets and strategic acumen that will lead the charge. When will we ever learn that we cannot *think* our way into the kingdom of God? And we can never *lead* our way into it either. We can only live our way into the kingdom of God by following the way of Jesus.

This does not mean that we turn our minds off. For several years I lived within a stream of Christianity that spiritualized everything from putting on socks to deciding where to eat lunch. Early on, one of the things that bothered me tremendously was the overspiritualizing of practically every situation. It was as if we had turned our brains in when we received the baptism of the Holy Spirit. On the other side of this approach are the streams of Christianity that overnaturalize, overanalyze, and overrationalize things. These are the many Christians and leaders who operate almost wholesale from the ability to reason and analyze through organization and social science theory. Now I am not against organization and planning. The problem comes when we cling to our plans and our own abilities to craft them. Human-made plans should always be held loosely.

CHURCH AS FACTORY

The Industrial Revolution ushered Newtonian approaches into just about every sphere of society. We surmised that we could figure everything out with a machinery approach. But the church is not a machine, and people are not parts. The only way the church is a business is that it is our heavenly Father's business. And he runs it with an otherworldly set of values, metrics, and means. The kingdom of God is his reign and rule. All of us are but citizens in his kingdom and must constantly recalibrate our motives and methods in relation to his.

The suffocating bureaucratic systems that drive factory-like churches stem from leaders obsessed with the search for predictable and controllable measures and outcomes. When it comes to churches, which are made up of people and everything about them—their skills, experiences, idiosyncrasies, faults, personalities, and so on—the Newtonian/mechanistic approach does not fit. And by the way, toss in that matter of the Holy Spirit and there is a serious monkey wrench in the works. Make no mistake—fear is what lies behind overly mechanized churches, ministries, and denominations. The fear of not being able to control outcomes is what creates these types of leadership structures and cultures. And the only places fear can abide are where faith is absent.

"Order" and "control" are not synonymous. Many controlling leaders will argue that they are merely seeking to provide order for their churches. Life is organic, but it is not void of order. Order is all throughout creation. Planet earth is finely tuned. Life, at every level, functions through precision, but the human race does not control it. In the instances where humans have attempted to alter landscapes by controlling agriculture and the like, disaster has often been the result. The infamous dust bowl of the 1930s across the American Southwest was caused by land being stripped for farming. God's order was displaced by the human pursuit of results through control. More recently, disastrous floods have occurred across mid-America because humans have dammed major rivers. Control in these cases brought about disorder and chaos.

Bringing people together as the body of Christ is rooted in the connectedness of relationships. This *is* God's order. Relationships cannot be controlled, and as to outcomes, they certainly cannot be predicted either. Church leadership cultures based on the corporate business world are invariably defined and navigated by boundaries of all kinds. In a machine, every piece has its place, and it must be kept in its place. Specific roles, responsibilities, lines of authority, and limits are created and instituted. Where this takes place relationship networks on the human level are circumvented and choked out and the power of God ceases to flow through the body of Christ. Very often people are deeply hurt in the process.

THREE

WIZARDS OF AAHS
THE HUBRIS OF LEADERDOM

Living out of the false self creates a compulsive desire to present a perfect image to the public so that everybody will admire us and nobody will know us.

—Brennan Manning[1]

The grosser manifestations of these sins, egotism, exhibitionism, self-promotion, are strangely tolerated in Christian leaders even in circles of impeccable orthodoxy. They are so much in evidence as actually, for many people, to become identified with the gospel. I trust it is not a cynical observation to say that they appear these days to be a requisite for popularity in some sections of the church visible. Promoting self under the guise of promoting Christ is currently so common as to excite little notice.

—A. W. Tozer[2]

My guess is that throughout history most little boys have imagined themselves as heroes. Oh, to be one of the great fire makers, dragon slayers, conquerors of minions, rescuers of damsels in distress, or caped crusaders of the day. Most of my childhood fantasies centered on my hero, Roger Staubach, quarterback of my beloved Dallas Cowboys. He was the real-life Captain America in my eyes. Barely a few square inches of wall space in my room were left uncovered by posters or newspaper clippings of Roger the Dodger. And it was rare for me to be without a No. 12 jersey on or a football in my hands. I wanted to be just like Roger and to grow up to be six foot three and marry a girl named Marianne. Surely someday I would be under center in Texas Stadium, late in the fourth quarter, raining down sixty-yard bombs on the hated Washington Redskins. The crowd would cheer, and following the game Tom Landry would utter appreciation for having such a great leader as old No. 12—Lance Ford.

American culture is especially in love with its heroes. We are ingrained with the belief that one guy (and it better be a guy) can save a city, a nation, or even a planet if need be. Our imaginations have been shaped by John Wayne, Rocky, Clint Eastwood, Indiana Jones, and the like—one-man wrecking crews who never fail to save the day. With a lit cigar in clenched teeth, the lone hero tells us to get out of the way and he'll lead us to the other side! This shaping myth has played a significant role in developing our ideas of leadership within the church as well.

Pick up just about any contemporary article or book on the subject of leadership and the language evokes the hero-leader persona. It strikes a chord with the little boy in all of us guys. "Yes! I may only be five foot ten and have only gotten into Texas Stadium because I bought a ticket, but I can still lead *my* team to victory. I have the opportunity to build something the way I have dreamed of doing it and to rally the troops around that dream, charge the hill, and take the city—for Jesus (of course)." Never mind that my name (as lead pastor) is plastered on mailings and marketing materials and that I am the fixture of most sermon promotions. "You've got it all wrong. This is all for the kingdom of God. It's not about me. It just looks that way. Actually, I am his humble servant. It's just that I can't show weakness. I know. It's complicated. You would have to be a leader to understand."

There is little doubt that some readers will say, "You're building a straw man and overstating the problem." My response is, not at all. We must wake up and take an honest look at the evangelical church. I may be describing a tin man but certainly not a straw man. We must take a hard look at ourselves. I have been around too many leaderoholics, plus I know what was in my own heart during the many years of my leaderdom obsession, to believe I am overstating the matter. Additionally, I have had dozens of conversations with others who have become aware of it in themselves. Add to that the scores of conversations I have had with those who are still fixated with the idea of the hero-leader as a primary pursuit, and there is no doubt that the problem is not overstated.

Bill Kinnon is a prolific blogger who recently touched on this issue as he reflected on the blog post of a mutual friend. The post he referred to centered on the graphically digitized image of a lone man, prodding through thick weeds and underbrush, unrolling what looked like an enormous tarp, but as it unfurled behind him, it became a road. Kinnon comments on the blogger's enthusiasm with the image:

He wrote this, "I absolutely love this image. . . . Visionaries do the hard work of **going ahead, going before and creating paths that no one else has thought about or dared to travel** [emphasis in original]." . . .

The image he professes to love leaves me cold. It's an image that fits with America's love of the mythic superhero. . . .

This is the myth of the rugged individual, and it is one . . . that has done more damage to the church in the west than we care to realize.[3]

Tocqueville's "rugged individual" label aptly fits the leadership model for the church of today. The ideal of a brave, singular church planter or great pastor is etched in the icon of lonely pioneers who braved the frontier dangers alone. Queue up the Indiana Jones theme. They are the conquering young warriors that fearlessly trek through uncharted territories to establish outposts and fortresses as they are on their way to becoming seasoned veterans and kings.

The progressive evolution of the ideal leader of a church in these molds has allowed a myriad of anti-Jesusian methods to be accepted across the evangelical landscape. As the church has simmered in the tainted pot of leadership stew, the very practices and attitudes that Jesus and the New Testament writers expressly forbade have spread like the black plague across the church world. It has become all about the one great leader, the king, the gospel knight in shining armor.

THE WAYS OF A KING

When Israel insisted on having a king to rule over them, the Lord gave in to their demands. But as he did so, he stressed a couple of things for the prophet Samuel to pass on to the people (1 Sam. 8). The first thing God wanted to make clear was that by making this choice the people of Israel were rejecting *the Lord* as their king (v. 7). To say, "We must have one man ruling over us," was tantamount to saying, "We don't want *you*, God, ruling over us." The Lord already had a leadership system in place. It was one that kept *him* front and center. He had already given them a king. But the people had better ideas.

Next, the Lord wanted Samuel to make it clear to the people of Israel what they were in store for from a ruling human monarch: "Now then, obey their voice; only you shall solemnly warn them and show them the ways of the king who shall reign over them" (v. 9).

Notice the phrase "warn them and show them the *ways of the king.*" Samuel obeyed God and proceeded to give a lengthy dialogue on how a king would build up his kingdom for his own interests through oppression and subjugation. Kings have a propensity for developing power structures to serve their own purposes. It is inevitable. A good-hearted king may come along every few generations, but a tyrant will emerge sooner or later. Even David—"a man after [God's] own heart" (13:14)—couldn't handle the power of the throne. He abused his authority in the most heinous of ways.

The request for a human monarch did not catch the Lord off guard. God knew beforehand that his people would reject his leadership and demand a king.

When you come to the land that the LORD your God is giving you, and you possess it and dwell in it and then say, "I will set a king over me, like all the nations that are around me," you may indeed set a king over you whom the LORD your God will choose. One from among your brothers you shall set as king over you. You may not put a foreigner over you, who is not your brother. Only he must not acquire many horses for himself or cause the people to return to Egypt in order to acquire many horses, since the LORD has said to you, "You shall never return that way again." And he shall not acquire many wives for himself, lest his heart turn away, nor shall he acquire for himself excessive silver and gold.

And when he sits on the throne of his kingdom, he shall write for himself in a book a copy of this law, approved by the Levitical priests. And it shall be with him, and he shall read in it all the days of his life, that he may learn to fear the LORD his God by keeping all the words of this law and these statutes, and doing them, that his heart may not be lifted up above his brothers, and that he may not turn aside from the commandment, either to the right hand or to the left, so that he may continue long in his kingdom, he and his children, in Israel. (Deut. 17:14-20)

Humanly held kingly power was never God's intention or ideal best for his people. In the passage above he strictly forbids returning to "Egypt" and "that way." This was a metaphor for the ways of the world—the domains of humans. ("The Egyptians are man, and not God, and their horses are flesh, and not spirit" [Isa. 31:3].) Toward the end of the passage the Lord warns of the king whose heart would be "lifted up above his brothers" (Deut. 17:20), which is exactly what happens when one man is set above all others. He begins to believe he is smarter, better, and more important than his brothers. The man who is king will begin to "acquire many horses" (v. 16)—a metaphor for turning to the ways of the flesh rather than relying on the Spirit of God and his word.

King Jesus is the only one fit to rule in the kingdom of God. He is the only one anointed to build and sit as Chief Shepherd (1 Pet. 5:4). Nevertheless, we have numerous phrases to justify our insistence on the idea of the single great leader:

- "The buck has to stop somewhere."
- "Only freaks have more than one head."
- "There has to be some*one* that makes a final decision."
- "Every team has to have a *head* coach."

"SENIOR" PASTOR

The majority of pastors I have discussed the subject with quickly dismiss the suggestion of any type of guidance in the church other than one guy at the top of the command chain. "I've never seen it work," they say. My argument is that *work* is exactly what it takes. It takes hard *relational* work for mutually submissive leadership to be successful. Denver pastor Kathy Escobar—who serves in a co-pastoring relationship—says,

For some reason I have always found myself attracted to the creative minority in the church. I feel connected to the dreamers and pot-stirrers who have ideas of toppling unhealthy power structures, practicing equality as a natural rhythm of life together, honoring doubt and questions, pursuing justice and mercy on behalf of others, and destroying the great divide between "us and them." On the whole, almost every system and structure we live in perpetuates power, strength and policy over relationship.[4]

In many ways it is certainly easier to just set up an organizational chart and make sure everyone stays within his or her boundaries. Institutions are always less messy than relationships. But institutions can never produce life. They can only contain it or fake it. The hard work of relationship building produces something that can never be concocted through committees and hierarchies. We will delve into the subject of mutually submissive leadership in depth in the second part of this book.

As I read the excellent Steve Jobs biography by Walter Isaacson, I came across a section where one of the people interviewed called Jobs a narcissist. Several times while reading the book the thought occurred to me that many of the traits—both good and bad—in Steve Jobs were ones I had seen in a multitude of pastors and church leaders. The narcissistic traits were especially noticeable, and that took me on a journey to understand more about the clinically defined narcissistic personality disorder (NPD).

It is somewhat dumbfounding when you consider the makeup of narcissists. Their behavior can be charismatic and charming one minute, cold and calculating the next, or occasionally given over to unpredictable rages.[5] I have to say that I read more books and articles on the subject than I could have imagined. Again, I found myself saying, "This stuff perfectly describes an inordinate number of pastors and church leaders I know personally and agrees with the many stories I have heard from those who have worked with them."

We are all somewhat narcissistic, whether or not we like to admit it. Though only about one out of a hundred people are clinically diagnosed with NPD, a large number of people are *deeply* narcissistic. And the leadership field draws them like ants to a picnic. Studies on the subject of NPD provide language and handles for us to gain a better understanding of what is going on in the orbit of the narcissistic leader. The following list is from a resource that professionals use for help in diagnosing NPD. Persons with NPD would have at least five of the following characteristics:

1. Have a grandiose sense of self-importance. They routinely overestimate their abilities and inflate their accomplishments, often appearing boastful and pretentious.

2. Often preoccupied with fantasies of unlimited success, power, brilliance, and beauty, or ideal love.

3. Believe that they are superior, special, or unique and expect others to recognize them as such. They may feel that they can only be understood by, and should only associate with, other people who are special or of high status and may attribute "unique," "perfect," or "gifted" qualities to those with whom they associate.

4. Require excessive admiration. This often takes the form of a need for constant attention and admiration.

5. A sense of entitlement is evident. They expect to be catered to and are puzzled or furious when this does not happen.

6. Sense of entitlement combined with a lack of sensitivity to the wants and needs of others may result in . . . exploitation of others. May expect great dedication from others and overwork them without regard for the impact on their lives.

7. Lack of empathy and difficulty recognizing the desires, subjective experiences, and feelings of others.

8. Often envious of others or believe that others are envious of them. May begrudge others their successes.
   . . .

9. Arrogant, haughty behaviors characterize these individuals. They often display snobbish, disdainful, or patronizing attitudes.[6]

LEADERSHIP IMMUNITY

I remember watching an episode of the television show *24* where Jack Bauer (there's the lone hero again) is helpless in his attempts to legally convict a foreign thug because the guy is protected under the statutes of diplomatic immunity. Since he is not bound to the laws of the host country, the foreign official is constantly able to get away with just about anything short of murder, based on his status as a diplomat. This is exactly what has happened in the matter of the king leadership myth. Staff members, church boards, and church members are turning their heads, looking the other way, holding hands over their ears, and providing safe passage for "great" leaders who are "getting the job done." These people are deemed to be so important and have built such legacies that we cannot muster the courage to call them out. They become untouchable.

Apparently this was the case at Penn State University, where the legendary Joe Paterno held court as head coach of the Nittany Lions football team for almost five decades. As a sex scandal involving one of Paterno's longtime coaches became public, so did stories of a culture at the school that gave a free pass to Paterno on almost every matter. JoePa, as he was known, was much more than a football coach. He was the czar of Penn State. Cross him and you cross out your own name as anything but mud at Penn State. Following his firing on the grounds that he failed to sufficiently act on a firsthand witness's account to him of a sexual assault on a child in his own locker-room showers, Penn State students rallied in his support while ignoring the most egregious of allegations that seemed strongly valid.

As I said above, in a later chapter we will dig in deeper as we look at the beauty and strength of the body of Christ living by mutual leadership. But for now it should be pointed out that this is one of the reasons that, in the wisdom of the Lord, we find no New Testament writer giving any grounds whatsoever for the lone-hero leader type. We have heard it our entire lives, "Power tends to corrupt, and absolute power corrupts absolutely."[7] Plain and simple, the human ego can't handle kingly power.

JESUS JERKS

For me, one of the most puzzling phenomena within Christian leaderdom is the toleration of what I call—I have no better way to say this—*Jesus jerks*. These are the pastors and leaders who, though admired by the crowds and masses, are known by their ministry staffs as . . . um . . . let's just say that Jesus rode into Jerusalem on one. These are the church leaders who display virtually no consistency in the fruit of the Spirit. You would be hard pressed to experience gentleness, kindness, patience, meekness, and the like from them on a regular basis. Sure, their public ministries evoke the *message* of the Bible, but their non-platform lives betray the state of their hearts.

My hope is that if you are a leader and the paragraph above, along with the coming pages in this chapter, describes you, that you will see it, acknowledge it to yourself, confess it to others, repent, take a sabbatical, and rebuild your character through Christ. If you serve on staff with a Jesus jerk, my intention is to point out that you are not imagining things. These folks exist, and they need to be called out. Such behavior should be given no safe haven in the body of Christ. Of all the scores of temptations possible, Satan uses two of the subtlest—pride and its progeny, arrogance—to entrap leaders. Though it seems clear that no sin could be more distinctly counter to all that Jesus was and is about, in Christian leaderdom, arrogance runs unabated like a free-flowing river.

Jesus is much more practical in his dealings with us than any of us can imagine. He waves away the fog, pushes the mirrors out of the way, and peels back the curtain to reveal the true state of the matter—the state of the heart. This was the thing that drove the religious leaders of his day crazy. In his predication of the dividing of the sheep from the goats (Matt. 25:31-33), Jesus emphatically declares that what we do, or fail to do, for others is what we do, or fail to do, for him. He says that the way we are with others is the way we are with him. So if you want to know how you are treating Jesus, just take a hard, honest look at how you are treating those around you.

Pastor, leader, listen closely. Your relationships with those on your staff is a spitting image of your relationship with Jesus—your faithful quiet time notwithstanding. The Jesus you are trying to get close to early in the morning is the same Jesus you berated yesterday afternoon. He is the same Jesus you pulled rank on a couple of days ago as you rudely interrupted and refused to listen to her side of the story. He is the Jesus that last week you fired, in the same way they would do it at "Sprint, or another business."

Over the last few years a new breed of young evangelical pastors has captured the imagination of thousands of young church planters. Often an arrogant tone and demeanor is cloaked as confidence in their God-given calling by many of the most well-known of this stream of pastors. Frequently I have watched online sermons where the phrase, "I don't care what you think of me," punctuates an especially strong preaching point. The words of C. S. Lewis nearly always echo in my mind when I hear such statements:

> Of course, it is very right, and often our duty, not to care what people think of us, if we do so for the right reason; namely, because we care so incomparably more what God thinks. But the Proud man has a different reason for not caring. He says "Why should I care for the applause of that rabble as if their opinion were worth anything?"[8]

LIMITLESS ENTITLEMENT

Narcissists often unwittingly ignore the separate existence of those around them. They behave as though the world revolves around them. In the case of hierarchical pastors it is their church world of which they themselves are the axis. Anyone south of them on the organizational chart is expected not only to jump at their beck and call but also to know inherently what they are calling for in the first place.

> It is as if you must live inside the Narcissist's head, share her thoughts and feelings, and be able to perform things that even she isn't able to do. Anything less is an affront to

her narcissistic sense of entitlement and need for perfect mirroring.[9]

The mythological character Narcissus was enamored with his own reflection. Narcissists likewise are obsessed with their own image and expect others to mirror them. Depending on the depth of their obsession they react with offense at the failure of others to render the reflection of their ways of doing things. Narcissists are so obsessed with their own image that, for good or bad, they believe everything in their world is a reflection of them. Read the following account from a friend that knew I was working on this book and thought I would find his story interesting:

> One of my best friends is the communications director at _____ church. Part of her job is to put together the weekly church bulletin, which is sent off to a printer in Florida who publishes it for free because it is now paid for by advertisements on the back page. Last Sunday she went to worship and then left to go visit her grandpa in the nursing home, [as] she does every Sunday. When she got out, she had four missed calls from a number at _____ church. She checked her voicemail, which had a frantic message from her overseer (an executive pastor). When my friend returned the call, the pastor asked her if she had seen the bulletin yet. She told her to turn to page 2, and my friend did. On page 2, there was supposed to be a box that read, "If you are visiting us today, please stop by the connecting booth for a free gift." Instead it read, "If you are visiting us today, please stop," in perfect, centered print. This was the funny part. The horrible part is that this pastor was freaking out and told my friend it was "her [hide]" if this was her fault. She (the executive pastor) said the senior pastor was "shaking, he was so mad" and refused to come out of his office. Apparently, in the main services, he offered profuse apologies to everyone for this "horrible mistake." My friend was able to show that she had sent a correct copy of the bulletin via PDF to the printer, so it was a printer error. But needless to

say, she shared the story to highlight how dismayed she was by the treatment of her "pastors." None of us could figure out why such a humorous situation during the Christmas season couldn't be enjoyed for the harmless mistake that it is, and this continues to highlight the fear and control that comes along with the corporate-attractional model.[10]

When dealing with an NPD individual you soon realize that there is a tremendous intolerance and sensitivity to anything less than a perfect performance. To fail to perform at the expected level is to trigger an outburst or fit of rage. When these episodes take place, it leaves the victim backing away to gain his or her bearings, just trying to make sense of what happened. It is especially shocking when it rampantly takes place in the body of the humble Servant, Jesus Christ.

The narcissistic leader really thinks it is all about him or her. Sure, he or she will claim otherwise: "I am seeking to bring God all the glory, and I am striving for us all to put forth our best for his sake." But those around this person know otherwise. I could easily share many stories of pastors who refuse to help church planters who feel called to start churches near their own churches. Some of these king-pastors even have new staff members sign agreements to never start new churches within a particular distance of their own churches. In the corporate world these are called noncompete agreements. It should be clear to any Christ follower that such action is insidious and heretical to the very witness of Christ. Pastors such as these are clearly building their own kingdoms, and the reality is that they are far from the kingdom of God themselves. The truth is that *they* are the ones in competition with God.

Narcissistic leaders view those around them as extensions of themselves. People are in place for *my* bidding. It is not hard to see how squirrelly things get when you have a king-leader in charge of a corporate business model of a church. People are looked at as tools, parts, and cogs. And they are considered to be as replaceable, with coldhearted ease, as a misfiring spark plug or burned-out fuse. The "user" makeup of narcissists who have power over others will consider any question of their authority or failure to agree or comply with their wishes as an all-out attack on who they are.[11]

ME WIN

The idea of win-win is a foreign notion for the narcissist. You would think that within the church, among "spiritual" leaders, that this would rarely be the case. Sad to say, but it all too often is precisely the case. Commenting on narcissists, clinical social worker Sandy Hotchkiss writes, "Mutuality and reciprocity are entirely alien concepts, because others exist only to agree, obey, flatter, and comfort—in short, to anticipate and meet my every need."[12] So if I am a narcissist and I cannot see you as useful for meeting my needs, then you are worthless and that's the way I will treat you. Furthermore, if you challenge what I want, get ready to feel my fury.[13]

If you have worked in a church with a pastor or upper-echelon leader such as the one just described, you know all too well what Hotchkiss is speaking of. Again, it seems almost untenable that such people are actually leading our churches. But they are—in spades.

Fresh out of Bible college in the mid-1980s, I found myself on staff at a church with a senior pastor who had a short fuse and a sharp tongue. My first staff experience had been with a pastor who oozed the Spirit of Jesus, so this was quite a shock for a fresh-faced twenty-two-year-old who assumed that church leaders usually acted like Jesus. After three or four months of not only being subjected to daily belittling and verbal abuse but also witnessing it happen to other staff members, I not so intrepidly approached the senior pastor on the matter of how he could treat us in such a way. He smirked, bit his bottom lip, then through clenched teeth said, "You guys come out of seminary and Bible college and expect churches to be all sweet and cozy. But this is the *real* world, and we are running a business here. You can't run a business and treat people like friends." He then went on to tell me that a friend of his—a very well-known

Houston pastor with a worldwide television ministry—would walk through his office every few months and arbitrarily fire a couple of secretaries for any reason he could come up with on the spot. The pastor told me he did this "just to keep them all on their toes." This senior pastor thought that was brilliant tactical leadership.

The most common rules of reciprocity do not come into play when dealing with an overly narcissistic leader. The only terms are the leader's terms. So-called leaders with a consistent demeanor such as this are not leaders at all. They are not even following Christ: "Do nothing from selfish ambition or conceit, but in humility count others more significant than yourselves. Let each of you look not only to his own interests, but also to the interests of others. Have this mind among yourselves, which is yours in Christ Jesus" (Phil. 2:3-5).

To follow Christ is to have the mind of Christ—to think like him. Jesus was of a mind that counted others more important than himself. He was of a mind that was beyond selfish ambition. Jesus was without conceit and went about looking out for the interests of others, jeopardizing his own reputation along the way. This is the mind of Christ. Followers of Christ think and act this way.

The main concern of the narcissistic king-leader is the preservation and expansion of his or her kingdom and importance regardless of the needs of others in the group. In his essays on the psychology of leadership, Manfred F. R. Kets de Vries writes,

> Their uninhibited behavior, self-righteousness, arrogance . . . and inability to accept a real interchange of ideas impair organizational functioning and prevent adaptation to internal and external changes. Their consequent exclusion of others from policy making, intolerance of criticism, and unwillingness to compromise inevitably have serious negative effects. . . .
>
> . . . Leaders driven by excessive narcissism typically disregard their subordinates' legitimate needs and take

advantage of their loyalty. This type of leader is exploitative, callous, and overcompetitive, and frequently resorts to excessive use of depreciation.[14]

I'M SO SPECIAL

Classic narcissists sincerely believe that TV's Mister Rogers was talking specifically to them. They believe that they are *especially* special. In church circles we have convenient labels to spiritualize and justify this vain perspective. The *call* or (especially in charismatic circles) the *anointing* is another way of saying, "I'm God's special guy." The idea of being special or "anointed" allows the king-leader to get away with all manner of anti-Jesus behavior.

Certain perks and privileges are usually reserved for the king-leader. This person comes and goes as he or she pleases, takes a day off here and there, and generally calls his or her own shots. On a daily basis this individual answers or reports to no one in particular. There is absolutely nothing wrong with this as long as this person gets the job done. The troubling issue is that (other than the executive pastor in some cases) the senior pastor is the only one who is allowed to operate this way. He or she is the only one deemed competent enough to self-manage. The other ministers are treated as employees. They are not *special*.

THE VISIONARY!

The leadership rhetoric over the last couple of decades has ushered in—in almost mythical proportions—the all-important, must-have, can't-do-successful-church-without *vision*. With the special king-leader comes vision. Make that *the* vision. The king-leader is tantamount to the queen bee. This person holds the special stuff inside that is key to the survival and expansion of the entire colony. Surviving and thriving is tied directly to this one individual.

Countless time and energy is spent on inspirational rhetoric and "vision casting" in order to motivate crowds and church staffs in support of the vision. Personal boundaries of staff members are constantly infringed on or outright ignored for the sake of the vision. Guilt and shame are common tools used by the king-leader to ensure that unhindered service is exacted from underlings. Late-night phone calls, interruptions on days off, barging in unannounced—the king-leader will do to staff members what they would never dream of doing. But again, this person is special, and the vision he or she brings is special. Hotchkiss writes,

> In such workplaces, people's private lives are cannibalized in the service of The Dream, and it is not unusual to see people putting in surreally long hours, sacrificing weekends and vacations, and coming to work sick. And they do it not just because they are afraid of losing their jobs, but also because their own emptied lives are inflated by their role in realizing the vision. The narcissistic fantasy captures the depleted in its net.
>
> This is not just the need to get the job done. Often the very nature of the job has been redefined in perfectionistic terms by the narcissistic leader, and this becomes the new standard of adequacy. It is no longer a matter of feeling good if you are able to live up to these expectations, it's about feeling bad if you don't. Grandiosity sets the standard, and shame befalls those who don't measure up.[15]

The leadership "vision" concept is nowhere to be found in the Gospels or the New Testament at large. We already have a vision and a visionary. Jesus and his kingdom are all we have and all we need. And he and it are more than enough. The vision myth is just that, a human-made, mesmerizing concept that diverts our attention from the simplicity of living out the gospel of the kingdom of God, being utterly dependent on *his* power, and making disciples along the way. That *is* our vision. This is not to say that individual faith communities and churches do not have unique calls in their particular contexts. They certainly do, and it is important for the members of those local churches to understand those particular God-given marching orders. My point is that the vision and the visionary idea are far beyond overemphasized and grossly hyped, cheered, and idolized.

WHY WE GO ALONG

So why do we allow narcissistic leaders to get away with the behavior we have talked about in this chapter? Why do we stay with them and why do we allow them to run over us all? King-leaders are most always extraordinarily charming in public. They are charismatic personalities who usually maintain an air of competence, savvy, and wit. They are the ones who light up the room when they walk in. No one seems to be as important or knowledgeable as him or her. Most of them have an almost theatrical air of confidence that is contagious. They have a knack for creating quick, superficial relationships. To be on their team makes us feel we must be special too. The narcissist in ourselves is flattered and emotionally supplied by being wanted by a *winner*. We should never forget that it was *the people* who wanted a king. And narcissists are always more than happy to oblige. They "feel they need to act out the fantasies created by their followers."[16]

Something almost magical seems to surround the aura of a "successful" leader or church. You feel you are part of something that is going somewhere. The place is special, and you don't want to miss out on it. Your own narcissistic tendencies are tapped again. As the church continues to grow, adds services, buildings, and multisite venues, you reason within that it must be God who is blessing it all and that *you* must be the one who is wrong. To allow critical thoughts against "God's man" or "God's woman" is tantamount to squaring off against the Lord himself. So you push those thoughts down and stay in the saddle.

When we go along with leaders like this, we are not honoring authority but enabling ungodliness. Our own codependence has seduced us. By warming ourselves in the glow of king-leaders and feeding from their buffet we are not only implicated in their sin but also signaling to abusive leaders our availability to meet their needs as they see fit. We become the posse for the thug.

Arrogance and pride are without fail telltale signs of insecurity. Many times it is a feeling of inner shame and a belief in the basement of a person's heart that he or she failed or didn't measure up to parental expectations that is behind the outward persona of the narcissistic king-leader. Psychologists believe that bypassed shame (i.e., suppressed) creates something of an empathy disconnect that allows aggressive impulses to go uncontrolled.[17]

In the heart of the narcissistic leader is a search for fulfillment outside the Lord. If such a person were secure in the Lord, he or she wouldn't be seeking fulfillment from others. This person would cease the relentless driving of himself or herself and others to meet his or her inward longing.

One former church staff member shares,

I remember a particular instance where the senior pastor popped into my office, unannounced. There was nothing confrontational about this specific encounter, but a few seconds after he walked out and closed the door I had an epiphany. I was suddenly aware of my sense of feeling like a little boy in the presence of an intimidating father. I reviewed the conversation I had just had with the senior pastor and realized that I was nervous and on edge. I found myself shrunk . . . wanting to appease him in every little way. Overall, I just felt reduced. I know the relationship this guy has with his dad. He is very intimidated by him and has never felt he can please him. He gets really uptight every time his dad comes into town. I realize that he is projecting onto the staff the very feelings he has for his father. He becomes like a little boy when his dad is around, and he makes guys like me do the same when he comes around us.[18]

The most egregious of these leader types will keep us locked into the roller coaster of their emotions. The ups and downs are the alternating strokes of our ego set against the sure-to-come pokes and put-downs from the king-leader. This contradictory up-and-down effect takes place inside the extreme narcissist. Unconsciously this person views himself or herself as inherently damaged and is ashamed because of it. On the flip side—the conscious side—this individual views himself or herself as an overcomer who has risen from the ashes and set the standard for others in his or her orbit to reach. Constant themes of perfection and excellence are projected onto others. Inevitably, shame and disappointment are released on others, who are consistently deemed incompetent and unable to do things right.

Eleanor Payson offers a list of questions to assist a person who suspects he or she may be involved in a personal or professional relationship with someone who has a narcissistic personality disorder.

1. Do you frequently feel as if you exist to listen to or admire his or her special talents and sensitivities?
2. Do you frequently feel hurt or annoyed that you do not get your turn and, if you do, the interest and quality of attention is significantly less than the kind of attention you give?
3. Do you sense an intense degree of pride in this person or feel reluctant to offer your opinions when you know they will differ from his or hers?
4. Do you often feel that the quality of your whole interaction will depend upon the kind of mood he or she is in?
5. Do you feel controlled by this person?
6. Are you afraid of upsetting him or her for fear of being cut off or retaliated against?
7. Do you have difficulty saying no?
8. Are you exhausted from the kind of energy drain or worry that this relationship causes you?
9. Have you begun to feel lonely in the relationship?
10. Do you often wonder where you stand in the relationship?
11. Are you in constant doubt about what's real?

12. Are you reluctant to let go of this relationship due to a strong sense of protectiveness?
13. Are you staying in the relationship because of your investment of time and energy?
14. Do you stay because you say to yourself the devil you know is better than the devil you don't know?[19]

NARCISSISTIC CHURCHES

Empire building is one of the manifestations of a narcissistic church, led by a narcissistic leader. Many churches have planted churches using the multisite model, and narcissistic churches follow this concept as a matter of franchising their "we're special" vision. This is not to say that all multisite churches are narcissistic. Not at all. Brothers Dave and John Ferguson, founders of Community Christian Church in Naperville, Illinois, have been significant shapers of the multisite church-planting phenomenon and are among the most humble and least narcissistic leaders you could ever hope to encounter. Community Christian has planted about a dozen churches in the Chicagoland area and beyond with no hint of franchising or control.

When a narcissistic leader plants a church or pastors one for a lengthy amount of time, the culture of the church will almost inevitably take on the personality of the king-leader. The "I'm special" syndrome pervades the self-perception of the staff and in many cases the church members. The vision of the church becomes perceived as the most significant vision in the city. Narcissistic churches rarely work in cooperative ministry or mission with the other churches in their communities, certainly not on a level playing field at any rate. The pride and hubris leading a church such as this will not be kept down but will inevitably appear, spilling over into whatever it touches.

PART II
BOARDING SERVANTSHIP

But whoever would be great among you must be your servant, and whoever would be first among you must be your slave, even as the Son of Man came not to be served but to serve, and to give his life as a ransom for many.
—Matt. 20:26b-28

INTRODUCTION
THE GREAT ONES AMONG YOU

Forcing someone to do something is just another way of controlling them. The key is to find a way to lead people without ruling them!

—Lebow and Spitzer[1]

We now move to the part of the book that points us in the direction we must head. It should be obvious by now that developing churches based on leadership takes us in a direction the Lord never intended us to go. Through a dizzying array of books, conferences, and web articles, we have been taught that everything rises or falls on leadership and that Jesus drew followers to himself in order to teach them to lead. Viewing Jesus through the lens of the Gospels, his language and actions do not support that notion. We observe Jesus gathering followers who he showed the way to become servants. Their leading was unto servantship.

If we look to Jesus as our mentor and model, we will only reach the conclusion that following him means seeking to be servants, not leaders. Then when we do lead, it is born from the person of Jesus. Our desire and greater obsession must be to develop servantship cultures in our ministries and churches. When we discover that serving is mentioned fifty times more in the New Testament than leading, we should need no more evidence of what is most pressing on the heart of God. And what presses God's heart must press ours as well.

The differences between servantship and leadership cultures are as contrasting as lush pastures and desert wastelands. There is little in common. People will say, "Well, of course we are to be *servant*-leaders. But leaders we must be." Over the past forty years the idea of servant leadership entered the church leadership conversation. But leaders could not bear the concept of "servantship" as a stand-alone term. "Leadership" had to be added to the equation.

Robert Greenleaf is credited with coming up with the term "servant-leader" in 1970.[2] His essay "The Servant as Leader" took hold across the landscape of business and educational institutions and continues to make a positive dent in some fields today where heavy-handed leadership typically prevails. As you read through this next part of the book, you will find that the term "servant-leader" is not used. It will be avoided because of the baggage—even toxicity—it sometimes carries. The word "servanthood" will also not be used for much the same reason. Both "servant-leader" and "servanthood" are watered-down terms that fall short of the necessary gumption to overcome the leader-centric mentality that saturates the church world. They are but twists on a vague notion of semi-humility. In many evangelical leadership cultures the idea of a servant-leader is in reality tantamount to a benevolent dictatorship.

If Jesus didn't choose to focus on leadership, why would we? If we discover that he focused heavily on servantship, why don't we? Jesus declared, "Among you it will be different" (Matt. 20:26, NLT). He says if we want to be first, we should go to the end of the line. If we want to be on top, hit our knees and get on bottom. For the one that aspires to be the greatest, assume the position of the least. According to Jesus the best results possible emerge when his followers choose to become his servants.

It is not necessary to focus on leadership, because his ethos of leadership is not a posture but a result. Let that sink in. Leadership is the fruit, not the tree. Jesus leadership just happens. Jesus tells us to *be* a servant. That *is* his form of leadership. Stop working to be a leader. *Be* a servant and people will follow your lead. We have been soaked in the concept that leadership must be fashioned, focused on, and purposely practiced. Jesus doesn't teach that at all. Jesus clearly—and repeatedly—modeled and instructed his followers to focus on and practice servantship.

Our quest of following Jesus into servantship must begin by asking, "Is it different among us?" For pastors, denominational executives, or other ministry staff members or overseers, the challenge is to ask that question about their personal way of leading and how it relates to the overall leadership culture of their church or organization. To discover the truth about ourselves we must ask a series of questions drawn from that first one:

- Do we do things differently around here?
- Do we use people?

- Do we treat people on our team differently from the way they would be treated if they worked in the corporate business sector? What about when someone on our team decides, or is asked, to leave? How are they treated? As they would be treated in a worldly business or differently?
- Does everyone have free access to everyone?
- Is information shared or guarded?
- Is the concept of collaboration rhetoric or reality?
- Can questions and challenges take place without fear of retribution or loss of favor?
- Do staff members have the same freedom and security that church members do when it comes to speaking up or speaking out?
- Are staff members treated like hirelings or co-laborers?

William Barclay observed, "God said to Jesus, 'Set up a reign of love.' Satan said to Jesus, 'Set up a dictatorship of force.'"[3] The "not so among you" declaration by Jesus pushes us into the reign of love—the domain of his kingdom—a *different* kingdom from the domain of humans.

UNLEARNING

Jazz great Dizzy Gillespie once said, "It's taken me all my life to learn what not to play."[4] To become an unleader necessitates an enormous amount of unlearning. It is tantamount to a drug addict or alcoholic going into detox and rehab. Our minds have become pickled in leaderspeak. We don't refer to church servants. We speak of church leaders. Have you ever heard of, much less attended, a servantship conference? The idea of being a servant is a downer to our flesh. The thought of becoming a better leader appeals to the inner ambition of most everyone.

When people—whether or not they are Christian—list the greatest people of the twentieth century, Mother Teresa is nearly always in the top five. Most people *admire* Mother Teresa, but who wants to really *live* like her? We love who she was, but we don't really want to do what she did. Mother Teresa was not a leader, but boy, did she ever lead. You may read those last couple of sentences and perceive a contradiction, as if hard-core servantship does not cause followers to emerge. This brings us to the hard-to-swallow issue of servantship.

There actually are people who want to do what Mother Teresa did. When she died, her Missionaries of Charity, which she began in Calcutta, had grown to over six hundred missions in over 120 countries. Mother Teresa would never have called herself a leader but simply a servant of Jesus. But did she lead? The answer is obvious. But what types of people follow Mother Teresa's lead? They are people who choose to follow the risk-it-all-give-up-my-life pathway and do as she did. It was the same way with Jesus. His disciples were what today we would call radicals. They abandoned ambition, careers, and family, everything the world values, for the sake of serving alongside Jesus. It is not that servantship does not produce followers. It does. But it produces a different type of follower. A servantship culture produces servants. Jesus and Mother Teresa created servantship cultures.

Everywhere you turn in church leadership discussions today the issue of discipleship abounds. "We are not making disciples. We're making consumers." "We must stop making church members and start making disciples." In those same conversations you will repeatedly hear, "We need more and better leaders, and we must lead differently ourselves." I cannot recall ever hearing a group of pastors in conversation say, "We need more and better servants. And we need to become better servants ourselves." The idea never even makes it to the table. We have not been ambitious about servantship. We have been hypnotized and fascinated with leadership.

Servantship changes everything. It changes attitudes and postures in the men and women who lead our ministries and churches. The tone and demeanor of a servant is altogether different from that of a leader. Servantship radically alters the culture and atmosphere when it is present. If you have ever taken a ship cruise, you know what a service culture is like. The job of the crew on a cruise line is to provide their guests with the highest possible level of service. The smiles and beckoning-to-every-call demeanor of the crew is overwhelming at times. When my wife and I took our three adult children and our son-in-law on a cruise to celebrate our twenty-fifth wedding anniversary, our son and son-in-law could not get over the fact that they could call room service at any hour, night or day, and have free food delivered by a smiling waiter.

Not only must we redefine "leadership" for the church, but we must also honestly redefine "servant." It seems rather obvious that when most of us church leaders apply the concept of serving to ourselves, it falls way short of the way we would define it in the real world. Let's go back to the cruise ship. The servers (a.k.a. waiters) live in rather spartan quarters, eat their meals after the guests have eaten theirs, and work extremely long daily shifts. The ship's captain—the chief—on the other hand, lives in a rather nice apartment-sized living space, has people who serve him, and enjoys many other perks.

Now think of your favorite superstar pastor. Do you honestly believe he or she is the most fervent servant in his or her church? Can you convince yourself that he or she has no more perks and privileges than others on the staff? If you are a senior pastor, executive pastor, or senior staff leader, answer honestly. Do you receive greater perks and privileges than nonsenior staff members?

Leadership Cultures
- Say, "Do what I say."
- Say, "I am the most valuable one here."
- Talk *to*.
- Work from rank.
- Decide based on who has the loftiest title in the room.
- Make threats and ultimatums.
- Are fear- and stress-filled.

Servantship Cultures
- Ask, "What do you think?"
- Say, "We are strongest together."
- Talk *with*.
- Work from role.
- Decide based on who makes sense in the moment.
- Make plans together.
- Are peace- and freedom-filled.

Some people are concerned that things will fall apart if leadership is not strongly emphasized. That fear is laughable. Did things fall apart for Jesus? Did Jesus get things done? Did Jesus have his "system" in good working order? Did Mother Teresa get things done? If we hope to change the world, we must become the servants Jesus wants us to be. Following the path of serving is to follow the path of Jesus. Grab your apron!

FOUR

ON BENDED KNEE
THE SERVANT'S SUBVERSION OF POWER

Wherever Christianity is, there is also self-renunciation, which is Christianity's essential form.

—Søren Kierkegaard[1]

He gave up his divine privileges; he took the humble position of a slave.

—Phil. 2:7, NLT

You're not a pastor. You're just a church builder." He meant it as a wake-up call, but Danny's words failed to penetrate me. About two years into the church I led the charge in planting, his increasing displeasure over the way our leadership system had developed left him both disappointed and angry. Danny had demonstrated mounting frustration over the past year, and it culminated in a meeting over coffee at my request where I asked him to leave our church. The chips on his shoulders were obvious to everyone in our growing fellowship, and his eye rolling and snide remarks had been steadily increasing over the previous weeks.

Danny had issues he needed to deal with in his own life, but that did not mean he was wrong about what he said to me as we parted. That was over sixteen years ago, and it probably took at least five years for me to actually *hear* what he was saying. He was right. It was not that I didn't love people. The problem was that I was more into building a church than I was into building the people who were the church. Like so many other church planters, I was consumed with developing my vision of church. And though I constantly preached that the church was the people, my obsession with developing the systems, organization, and expansion of our church betrayed what I really believed in the basement of my heart. I was a leader, not a servant. I was building a leadership culture, not one of servantship. Not one of followership.

In our attempts to create Jesus in our own image we often think of him as a great leader. Many pastors have read the Laurie Beth Jones book *Jesus, CEO*. But neither Jesus nor God ever labeled him as such. No, Jesus was a great servant—the greatest servant of all—and he embraced the status of a servant: "Behold my servant, whom I uphold, my chosen, in whom my soul delights; I have put my Spirit upon him" (Isa. 42:1).

Jesus' focus was not on building a great organization or system. His building of the church was through planting and building relationships through an intrinsic recognition of other people's worth. Authentic relationship requires mutual initiative to sustain it. When one person has greater authority or status, he or she usually must initiate the relationship. This is where servantship played its part in Jesus' modus operandi. From little children to despised tax collectors, from lepers to prostitutes, Jesus built relationships with the most ordinary of people. He took the leftovers the religious leaders deemed unfit to invest in. To do so Jesus had to divert the attention from his growing status and fame. He was "the stone that the builders [the religious elite] rejected" (Matt. 21:42), and he would take these plain-as-rock people, whom the religious elite also rejected, and turn them into "living stones" (1 Pet. 2:5). Their cumulative lives were the material from which he would build his church.

Depending on the translation, at the very most, "leader" is used only six times in the New Testament, while the word "servant" can be found over two hundred times. We should be asking why those of us who have a calling to serve the church obsess so much more over leadership than servantship. Jesus said, "I am among you as the one who serves" (Luke 22:27). If we honestly want to be like Jesus—if we honestly want to follow Jesus—we will pursue servantship rather than leadership. We will work to become the greatest servants we can be.

The apostle Paul understood this from the depths of his redeemed being. It is quite obvious, as his favorite designation for himself was the word "servant." He opens up his epistle to the Romans by declaring himself to be not a leader but a "servant" (1:1)—and not just any typical servant. The word Paul chose as his favorite label for himself was the Greek word *doulos*, which means "bondslave." A *doulos* is a slave who has given up his freedom and will. New Testament scholar Kenneth Wuest writes, "The word . . . *doulos*, [was] the most abject, servile term used by the Greeks to denote a slave. The word designated one who was born as a slave, one who was bound to his master in chords so strong that only death could break them, one who served his master to the disregard of his own interests, one whose will was swallowed up in the will of his master."[2]

I can just imagine Paul's bio if he were to speak at one of the large leadership conferences today. It would most likely read something like this: "Paul, formerly known as Saul of Tarsus, is an at-large janitor for Jesus. He is the property of Christ and has no purpose other than to be a slave, without personal rights of his own."

WHY LEADERSHIP CULTURES MUST FALL

Leadership cultures do not possess the cultural intelligence for genuine community. They will always fail to bring about genuine unity. They draw their cues from the system of this fallen world. Jesus observed that this was the way the Gentiles operated (Matt. 20:25). Hierarchy was an immediate result of the fall of humanity. The man began to rule over the woman, and the first hierarchical culture had begun. But servantship cultures emerge from the upside-down ways of the kingdom of God. Gilbert Bilezikian writes,

> The human uprising against God that we call "the Fall" wreaked havoc on the neat arrangement God had implanted in the Garden of Eden. God's design for ministry as participatory stewardship was turned on its head by the entrance of sin on the human scene. Whereas a servant-to-servant relationship had originally prevailed among humans, the Fall brought about a ruler-servant relationship (Gen. 3:16). Within such a structure of hierarchy, participation in communal tasks became subject to the will of the individual holding authority over the community.[3]

The plan of God was to make the Israelites an entire nation of priests, serving the world on his behalf (Exod. 19:6). His will was to be their one and only King. But the people refused to accept or be satisfied with God as King. Eventually a human monarchy was set in place at the request of the people, against the advice of God, who warned them how it would eventually turn out. It is rather ironic that the Lord again has tried to be the King of his people, whom he wants to be a priesthood of believers (1 Pet. 2:9), serving the world. But just like Israel under the old covenant, most of the church has demanded a monarchy. God is rejected as the Chief Ruler of the church.

When we accept the position of God's bondslaves, we pick up his assignment of becoming the servant of others. This is where the hard part comes in. I don't mind serving God. I jump at the opportunity to do that. To serve God is an honor and a privilege. The problem is that God says, "Yes, I want you to serve me. Now, here is what I want you to do. Go over there and serve so-and-so." Once we agree to be God's slave, he gives us the assignment of serving other humans. And humans do not treat servants and slaves well.

One of the most difficult parts of relationships with people lies not in valuing others but in *demonstrating* our value for others. It is incumbent on a servant that he or she show respect and honor for the dignity of the one he or she is serving. We're talking real, genuine respect here. A servant in a king's palace shows deep respect to the king, even when he or she disagrees with the decisions or direction the king is taking. A servant honors the dignity of the office of the king. This is the same posture we are to take with one another. A king's servant also must show respect to the king's guests. Those guests may quite often be rude, demeaning, and unappreciative of the service of the servant, but the servant continues to serve. "Service with a smile," the saying goes. On the outside the servant may be serving the jerky guest, but on the inside he or she is serving *for* his Master, his Lord.

In the first half of this book we focused on church leadership structures that trample the dignity of fellow servants. It is inexplicable that so-called church leaders, pastors, and denominational higher-ups can read the Bible often and study the life of Jesus and yet degrade and intimidate others. There should be no occasion in which we fail to honor the dignity of and express value for the *imago Dei* (image of God) in others. These values are not to be tossed out when it comes to the culture of a church staff. The only way they possibly can be pitched is if we hang on to the ways of the Gentiles by constructing leadership cultures with organizational charts that rank certain people above others and then set in place a system of command and control to manage those people. Of course, this is exactly what has taken place.

I have little doubt that some leaders currently reading this are wondering—maybe even saying out loud—"How else are we to run a church?" That is the point. We are not to "run a church." As we will see in the forthcoming chapters, what we have called church "staffs"—a term borrowed from the ways of the Gentiles—are to be collectives of called men and women who understand their roles and work together in mutual submission, with Jesus as their one and only Chief Shepherd. The major reason some leaders can hardly conceive of such a concept is because they cannot imagine a group of people being able to self-manage—although every top-dog, senior pastor I have ever met believes he or she has the ability and right to self-manage and is nonplussed with anyone who would suggest otherwise.

For some reason most senior pastors believe they are the only ones who have the right to be trusted to self-manage. But unleaders—working from cultures of servantship—operate from a stance of mutual submission. This neutralizes and limits the hoarding and abuse of power. Kathy Escobar says, "Hoarding power won't work on the downward descent. We will have to learn to diffuse power, which sometimes looks like giving it away, but sometimes looks like stepping into the responsibility of it. Diffusing power means inviting others to share leadership, value and voice. Diffusing power means moving away from one leader and hero worship, to finding ways to include and make room for others, and continually fan into flame people's gifts and passions."[4]

Trusting the servantship heart in others around us is an essential ingredient of a humble church culture. To fail to trust and give release to our fellow servants is to stand on the platform of pride, believing that without our control of others and the overall game plan for the church, success will escape our faith community as a whole. This does not negate accountability. It actually enhances it. Accountability becomes mutual, as does the concept of submission.

THE WAY OF HUMILITY

Giovanni Francesco di Bernardone was born into a wealthy family, with all the accruements of financial wherewithal. Status and power surrounded his daily life and personal world. Yet he chose to abandon it all by choosing to follow Jesus in the most literal way he knew to do. History remembers Giovanni as Francis of Assisi, the founder of the Franciscans. Differing from the Benedictines, who withdrew from society to live a cloistered life of solitude, the Franciscans lived a very public life among the poor of their host culture. Francis could have taken an easier route, but he chose not to parlay his inheritance into a funding stream for his ministry. He abandoned his inheritance. Turning his back on the power and status at his disposal, Francis chose the posture and identity of a servant. He chose Jesus as his model of servanthood, and what he started continues to affect the world in a positive way, centuries after his death.

Scott Bessenecker writes, "The hope for the world lies in meekness. Jesus said, 'Blessed are the meek, for they will inherit the earth' (Matthew 5:5). The reason that the meek will inherit the earth is that they are naturally disposed to use power in the way it was designed by God to be used—as a guard for the weak and to preserve the common good."[5] Jesus was constantly not only bringing tangible healing to people but focused on the inner person as well. He valued people over projects, processes, and systems. Oswald Sanders speaks of the heart of Jesus as he showed himself as an example for his followers: "Only once in all the recorded words of Jesus did our Lord announce that he would provide an 'example' for the disciples, and then he washed their feet (John 13:15). Only once in the rest of the New Testament does a writer offer an 'example' (1 Peter 2:21), and that is an example of suffering. Serving and suffering are paired in the teaching and life of our Lord. One does not come without the other. And what servant is greater than the Lord?"[6]

At the heart of servantship is the love for the other. The tangible, practical service we enter into when we come across people or situations that need healing, redemption, or justice often necessitates the humbling of ourselves to get into position to help. People who are down on their luck need others to get *down* with them in order to help. A lifeguard cannot save a drowning person from his lofty perch. He must dive deep. He must go down.

Few people are not touched when they hear the national anthem of their homeland, especially when it is played at an Olympic medal ceremony or sung prior to a sporting event. For many Americans, Jimi Hendrix's guitar version of "The Star-Spangled Banner" in 1969 at Woodstock comes to mind as memorable. And Whitney Houston's rousing rendition at the Super Bowl in 1991 is perhaps the most celebrated version of America's national anthem. But you will be hard pressed to find a more touching version than the one witnessed on April 27, 2003, prior to game four of the National Basketball Association playoffs between the Dallas Mavericks and the Portland Trail Blazers.

Professional athletes live for the playoffs. Beyond the fame and money that comes from being one of the very few people who ever get to be paid to play, the pursuit of a championship ring sits atop the most cherished of dreams for professional ballplayers. The playoffs represent the first step to a possible championship. The playoffs are winner take all and sudden death for the loser.

Though the average citizen will hear the national anthem only a handful of times in a given year, a professional basketball player has heard it eighty-two times by the time the playoffs come around. His mind is focused on the game, and it is understandable if the song blends in as nothing more than a pregame ritual to get past in order to get down to the important thing, the game.

So just imagine you are Maurice Cheeks, the young coach of the Portland Trail Blazers. This is what you have been working for your entire life. Your career, your reputation—everything is on the line. This is your moment, and your mind is focused on the strategy of the game and how it will unfold—the necessary moves you and only you can make as a leader. But first, the national anthem.

Stepping onto the court is a thirteen-year-old girl named Natalie Gilbert. She had won a local singing contest and was invited to sing the national anthem prior to this important game. Natalie appeared a bit shaky as she began but started the song out on key and seemed to be doing just fine—when *it* happened. The nightmare every singer dreads. Natalie forgot the words. Trying to squeeze out a smile, with a wavering voice, she butchered the lines and suddenly stood silently with the microphone shaking in her hand. Struggling not to burst into tears she turned around as if looking for someone to help her. With millions of people watching on television and thousands others in the arena, Natalie stood completely alone—but only for a few seconds.

Dropping his game plan, Maurice Cheeks jogged from his position alongside his team and joined Natalie. This giant of a man, a former four-time NBA all-star himself, placed one hand on her left shoulder, used his other hand to steady her shaking hand that held the microphone, leaned over her, and began to sing. At his urging and with his accompaniment Natalie began to sing too. Quivering at first but growing confident as the song progressed, she sang her heart out. Interestingly enough, Maurice Cheeks cannot sing a lick. He was off-key for the entire song. But it didn't matter. There was no Randy Jackson around to care that he was pitchy. No one had ever heard "The Star-Spangled Banner" sung so wonderfully. The entire arena joined in singing at the top of their lungs, and at the end of the song the place erupted in applause as fireworks rained down. With a huge smile of relief, Natalie looked up at her hero and said, "Thank you." Maurice Cheeks humbled himself and became a servant to a little girl who was in a crowd, alone, and in trouble. He taught millions the Jesus way of leading—by serving. Maurice Cheeks lived out the words of the apostle Paul:

> Do nothing from selfish ambition or conceit, but in humility count others more significant than yourselves. Let each of you look not only to his own interests, but also to the interests of others. Have this mind among yourselves, which is yours in Christ Jesus, who, though he was in the form of God, did not count equality with God a thing to be grasped, but emptied himself, by taking the form of a servant, being born in the likeness of men. And being found in human form, he humbled himself by becoming obedient to the point of death, even death on a cross. (Phil. 2:3-8)

To assume the position of servant is a necessary aspect of Jesus' commandment for us to pick up our crosses each day if we claim to be his disciples. Laying our lives down for others is manifested in the small sacrifices, as well as in the more dynamic ones. The reality is that opportunities for spectacular deeds of sacrifice do not come along very often, but opportunities for small sacrificial acts present themselves every day. Slowing down to let someone else get ahead of you in the lunch line or deflecting credit to another co-laborer can be a simple act of servantship that comes from nailing your pride to the cross. This is what it means to enter and live into the kingdom of God. Author John Dickson says, "Humility is the noble choice to forgo your status, deploy your resources or use your influence for the good of others before yourself. More simply, you could say the humble person is marked by a willingness to hold power in service of others."[7]

THE DESTRUCTIVE SPIRIT

The idea that Christian leaders would hold on to status and rank should be scandalous in our eyes. We should be left totally dumbfounded when we try to understand how it is possible for Christian leaders, from pastors to seminary presidents, to continue to walk in arrogance and pride. Arrogance and Jesus don't mix. One would think that if we truly believe we are living in the presence of the risen Christ, his presence alone would be humbling enough. Rarely is it the case. Surely we are all carrying a certain measure of pride. C. S. Lewis argued that if we say we are not conceited, that is the very proof we are conceited. I have no doubt of this fact in myself. The hard lesson of pride is that we will always eventually have to pay the rent on it. Pride does not make a place for us for free. If you refuse to let go of pride, you will pay for it. It is not an *if* but a *when* scenario: "Pride goes before destruction, and a haughty spirit before a fall" (Prov. 16:18).

In his groundbreaking best seller *Emotional Intelligence* Daniel Goleman tells the story of Melburn McBroom, an airline pilot with a reputation as an intimidating and domineering leader. On a fateful day in 1978, on approach to landing in Portland, Oregon, McBroom noticed a problem with the plane's landing gear. He set the plane in a holding pattern, circling the airfield while he checked on the problem. Goleman writes, "As McBroom obsessed about the landing gear, the plane's fuel gauges steadily approached the empty level. But his copilots were so fearful of McBroom's wrath that they said nothing, even as disaster loomed. The plane crashed, killing ten people."[8] This tragic story has become a cautionary tale that has revamped flight-crew training for most major airlines. Unfortunately, the truth of Prov. 16:18 all too often comes to roost. The apostle Paul said, "Knowledge makes arrogant" (1 Cor. 8:1, NASB).

GOING *DOWN* TO THE PROMISED LAND

After forty years of aimlessly wandering in the desert of Sinai the children of Israel finally were within reach of the Promised Land. Four decades of trial, heartache, and exile would be over in a matter of minutes. Their eyes were on the place of their dreams, but their feet remained in the desert. Just one more obstacle remained. Situated between the Israelites and the land of milk and honey was the Jordan River. They would have to cross it to enter into the Land of Promise.

The Jordan River represents a life lesson for us all. The name "Jordan" in Hebrew means "going down" or "bent knee." When commoners approach royalty, they prostrate themselves by either lying flat on the ground or positioning themselves on bended knee with head bowed. This posturing uses the entire body to send a message of complete submission to the one in authority.

When in his discourse, known as the Sermon on the Mount, Jesus stated, "The meek . . . shall inherit the earth" (Matt. 5:5), undoubtedly his audience would have immediately recognized it as a quotation from Ps. 37: "But the meek shall inherit the land and delight themselves in abundant peace" (v. 11). Practically every modern translation renders the word "earth" as "land" in this psalm. The Jewish people of the day clearly understood this as a reference to the Promised Land.

As in so many eras throughout their history the Israelites of Jesus' day found themselves under the thumb of an oppressive regime. The Roman shadow of power and suppression hovered over the daily lives of the Jewish people. With hopeful eagerness they looked for their deliverer to free them from the tyranny of the Roman emperor and empire, just as the Israelites in the days of Moses had done so many years before, longing to be delivered from their Egyptian overlords.

Surely this Jesus who stood before them—the One who so many hearers declared spoke with authority and who had displayed before them his miracle-working power—surely he was the eagerly awaited deliverer. And certainly he would use his authority and power to defeat and sack the sorry Romans once and for all. Astonishingly, Jesus declared no such thing—at least in no such way.

Jesus probably bummed his audience out when he said, "The meek—the humble ones who bend the knee—will be the ones who enter the Promised Land." Can you imagine the reaction throughout the crowd? "What! The meek? You have got to be kidding!" Jesus was constantly dropping these types of counterintuitive kingdom bombs. Questions must have been flying like rockets. "You mean you're not going to rain down fire and brimstone? No plagues? No earthquakes? No angels on white horses?" This principle stands true today. The kingdom of God is entered into through a posture of humility.

The first time we hear of the disciples jockeying for position is in Matt. 18:

> At that time the disciples came to Jesus, saying, "Who is the greatest in the kingdom of heaven?" And calling to him a child, he put him in the midst of them and said, "Truly, I say to you, unless you turn and become like children, you will never enter the kingdom of heaven. Whoever humbles himself like this child is the greatest in the kingdom of heaven." (Vv. 1-4)

The disciples asked, "Who is the greatest in the kingdom of [God]?" After all, they lived in a culture of hierarchy. From the Romans to their own Jewish religious leaders, the disciples lived in a society with a heavy-handed ruling class structure. Everyone was trying to climb the ladder of stature and success. But Jesus had been modeling an entirely upside-down way. The question, "Who is the greatest?" exposed what was in the hearts of the disciples. It revealed they were still clueless about the nature of the kingdom of God and about the hearts of those who would gain entry into it.

Notice carefully Jesus' words, "Unless you turn . . ." (v. 3). The only reason to tell someone to turn around is so that person can find what he or she is looking for. Jesus was telling his disciples that they were headed in the wrong direction. They were focusing on the very opposite of what he wanted them to focus on. The disciples were actually moving away from the kingdom of God rather than toward it. When we are driving to fulfill personal ambition and prestige, to acquire ever more notoriety and power, along with exaltation, we are going in the opposite direction of Jesus and the kingdom of God. We are actually headed deeper into the kingdoms of the human race. When we focus on our own status, we have turned our backs on the kingdom of God.

It is not enough to turn around. It is possible to turn around and head in a different direction while still being unchanged in our hearts. Jesus says to turn around and become like children. He didn't say it was optional either. "Unless you turn and become like children, you will never enter the kingdom of heaven" (v. 3). Jesus then goes on to connect back to the disciple's original question. "Oh, you want to know how to be the greatest? Okay, do this. Become like this child." Then Jesus tells the Twelve how to do it. He says they must humble themselves.

If you visit the Church of the Nativity in Bethlehem, you will discover the main access to it is by a very small passageway called the Door of Humility. It is a reminder that Jesus was born and is still incarnated in humble settings. In order to get to him, we must get low. Jesus shows up in the midst of humility. There is only way to become humble. You have to do it yourself. We must humble ourselves. Other people can humiliate us, and at times we accidentally humiliate ourselves. That does not necessarily make us humble. It is up to us to humble ourselves. The word "humble" is the translation of a Greek word meaning "to take a lower rank and become plain." These are astounding words. Jesus says that the key to breaking into the kingdom of God is to take the lowest rank. It means we become *plain*. We are to fade into the crowd.

NOT TO BE SERVED

At the very top of his game, entering into the sweet spot of fame and adulation as a world-renowned writer and speaker, Henri Nouwen set aside his position of notoriety and joined Daybreak, a community for people with developmental disabilities in Toronto. His peers were astonished that Nouwen would lay down his position of power to pick up a task that "anyone" could do. His experience at Daybreak became a significant shaper of Nouwen's final years, as well as an immeasurable influence for some of his most treasured writings.

To settle for the weedy fields of leadership on our journey of following Jesus is like lodging in a Route 66 trailer court when we could have been camping in Yellowstone. We miss out on the glorious grandeur of God's creative splendor in others. Servants do not get served. They serve. Oswald Sanders writes, "We do not read about 'Moses, my leader,' but 'Moses, my servant.' And this is exactly what Christ taught. Jesus was a revolutionary, not in the guerilla warfare sense, but in his teaching on leadership. The term *servant* speaks everywhere of low prestige, low respect, low honor. Most people are not attracted to such a low-value role. When Jesus used the term, however, it was a synonym for greatness. And that was a revolutionary idea."[9]

My buddy Brad Brisco and I cofounded a yearly conference that takes place in Kansas City where some of the most well-known leaders, thinkers, and authors in the evangelical church present talks around the subject of everyday Christians living out the mission God has assigned them. One of the most talked-about aspects of our conference revolves around what we call "living rooms." This idea came about from my own angst with what I had witnessed for many years taking place at Christian leadership conferences. Every conference I had spoken at or attended had a "green room," a concept that comes from the entertainment industry. A green room is a lounge for actors and performers to relax in before they go onstage to perform. They are safe hideouts for the stars to be alone or among the other stars.

When Brad and I began thinking about the ethos and atmosphere of our conference, we wanted to eliminate any hint of hierarchy. We informed each guy and gal that would be speaking at the conference about our "living rooms." These are hangout spots set up in the open common area of the conference venue. They have couches and club chairs for the speakers to hang out with all the conference attendees. It sets the tone for what we believe about leadership—that none of us are *leaders*. It is just that at times we *lead*. So when a speaker is on the platform doing his or her talk, he or she is leading; when a speaker is finished with the talk, he or she is *among* the body. The person is thus not a leader but a fellow servant.

I will never forget the first time I laid my eyes on a speaking contract for a Christian event. I was in my early twenties, working on a small conference at the West Texas church I was serving. A famous Christian rock group was part of the lineup, and their agent sent the contract for me to sign. Within the contract was the section referred to as a rider. For an entertainer or performer this addendum typically spells out particular demands for serving the entertainer. I could not believe my eyes as I looked at what these "servants" were demanding. It was all spelled out in detail: Five cans of Diet Coke, five cans of Dr. Pepper, six bottles of Perrier mineral water, one two-pound bag of Skittles candy, and on it went. I was shocked.

I tried to put the incident out of my mind, saying to myself that these were just musicians and that they were just immature in their Christianity and didn't realize what they were doing. That was until I held in my hands the contract of a famous preacher I had long admired. He was to be our keynote speaker, and a few days after receiving the contract for the band I received a contract from his assistant as well. I stood in stunned disbelief as I read it. This "servant of the Lord" required not only a first-class airline seat but also a particular seat within first class. The contract also spelled out explicitly that under no circumstance was he to be transported in a church van or a vehicle other than a newer four-door sedan. That was over twenty-five years ago, and I know for a certainty that this type of scenario continues to abound throughout evangelical Christianity today. We are reminded of Jesus' words again: "The Son of Man came not to be served but to serve" (Matt. 20:28).

Like Henri Nouwen, Albert Schweitzer stunned his academic colleagues by abandoning a successful academic career to spend seven years earning a medical doctorate in order to work as a medical missionary in Gabon, West Africa. In his memoirs, Schweitzer attempts to bring clarity to the thinking behind the sacrificial choices he made:

Only a person who can find a value in every sort of activity and devote himself to each one with full consciousness of duty has the inward right to take as his object some extraordinary activity instead of that which falls naturally to his lot. Only a person who feels his preference to be a matter of course, not something out of the ordinary, and who has no thought of heroism, but just recognizes a duty undertaken with sober enthusiasm, is capable of becoming a spiritual adventurer such as the world needs. There are no heroes of action: only heroes of renunciation and suffering. Of such there are plenty. But few of them are known, and even these not to the crowd, but to the few. Of those who feel any sort of impulse, and would prove actually fitted, to devote their lives to independent personal activity, the majority are compelled by circumstances to renounce such a course. Those who are so favored as to be able to embark on a course of free personal activity must accept this good fortune in a spirit of humility. They must often think of those who, though willing and capable, were never in a position to do the same. And as a rule they must temper their own strong determination with humility.[10]

POWER—JESUS STYLE

True to the form of the dynamics of the upside-down kingdom of God, the apostle Paul makes the counterintuitive statement that God's power is formulated and perfected in Paul's own weakness. He continues to say that his greatest boast is in his own weaknesses so that the power of Jesus may come upon his life: "But he said to me, 'My grace is sufficient for you, for my power is made perfect in weakness.' Therefore I will boast all the more gladly of my weaknesses, so that the power of Christ may rest upon me" (2 Cor. 12:9).

Missiologist Jayakumar Christian says, "The challenge before the church is the transformation of the very nature of power."[11] To encounter the kingdom of God is to encounter the rule of God, the power of God. The Lord challenges all god complexes. Power in the kingdom of God in the lives of his servants is incubated in their willingness to acknowledge and even embrace their own weaknesses.

Jesus was (and still is) a liberator. His spirit moves through the kingdoms of humanity, redeeming and transforming people and rebuking and ejecting principalities and powers. Worldly systems and structures were endangered species when Jesus came into the neighborhood. The Gospels record a multitude of occasions when Jesus broke down hierarchical structures that blocked relationships between people and God. His liberating judgment was aimed at all forms of oppressive entitlement at the hands of the religious elite. Jesus attacked the way the religious leaders used the Sabbath as a tool of oppression over the Jewish people. He was constantly eating with sinners and performing miracles and healings especially on the Sabbath to call out and provoke the scribes and Pharisees to a showdown. The kingdom of God always threatens the power of those with vested interest in a particular structure. When we cherish our systems more than we cherish people and God's mission, we lose the power to be changed ourselves, much less to change the system itself.

Manifestations of power in Jesus' ministry confound the world's concepts of power. He redefined power in a myriad of ways. From the towel and basin with which he washed his disciples' feet to the act of giving himself up to the cross, his strength manifested in acts that humanity defined as weakness. Jayakumar Christian writes,

> Jesus went further than just ignoring the lines that have divided people since the beginning of human history. Jesus not only mixed with the poor intentionally, but he angered the religious leaders by making his association with the sinners a religious issue. For Jesus, this erasing of the lines was integral to his understanding of mission. God's kingdom challenges those lines, not just because of God's special concern for the poor, but because those lines are contradictory to the reign of God. The kingdom of God challenges the power of oppressors to divide and rule.[12]

It is not an overstatement to claim that Jesus detested boundaries that hinted at prestige and status. He called out the scribes in front of all the people for their love of sitting in "places of honor at feasts" and reserving the "best seats [for themselves] in the synagogues" (Luke 20:45-46). I can't help but think of this when I see special reserved parking places at church buildings for pastors. That may seem like a tiny thing, but it is actually a very telling thing. The kingdom of God is a society void of prestige and status among men and women. There is to be no hint of division that establishes status between the inferior and superior. The very character of authority and power for the world's system is demonstrated through domination. It is the arrogance of people playing on the fears of others that creates structures of hierarchy, domination, and exploitation. Jesus held these and other distortions of power up to total ridicule.[13]

Few people have addressed the issue of humility with the insight of the legendary C. S. Lewis. This chapter would certainly be wanting if we were not reminded of his wisdom on the matter. In Lewis's thinking God forbids pride, not because it infringes on his dignity, but for an especially important reason:

> He wants you to know Him: wants to give you Himself. And He and you are two things of such a kind that if you really get into any kind of touch with Him you will, in fact, be humble—delightedly humble, feeling the infinite relief of having for once got rid of all the silly nonsense about your own dignity which has made you restless and unhappy all your life.[14]

FROM SELF TO SERVANT

I recently watched a humorous video of a little boy who, for the first time, discovered his shadow. He became extremely frustrated that he could not get away from it. Try as he might his shadow followed him everywhere. The little guy even squatted down and tried to pound the shadow away with his fists. Finally, he turned and ran screaming. It was not until he made his way into the bigger shadow of the nearby trees that his own shadow finally dissolved away. Personal ambition and the acquisition and use of power are much like the little boy and his shadow. Until we turn and run into servantship, personal prestige and the exalting of self will manifest their darkened forms everywhere we show up. These characteristics of the fallen ways of the human race must be absorbed into the meekness of servantship found within the kingdom of God.

The servant of God subverts the power of human ways through one chief means—meekness, humility. This means will manifest in differing ways as the occasion demands. As I wrote this chapter, I sat back at one point and tried to think of who I was personally acquainted with that personified my imagination of the Jesus type of humility. Three men in particular came to mind. Each of these guys has a different personality. But as I thought about each of them, I realized that each one is also a powerfully gifted man of God. Each of them possesses a gentleness that is tempered by a solid dose of authority. But it is not an imposed authority. It is the type of authority that you want to lean into, to join in with. I then read the words of C. S. Lewis that gave an apt description:

Do not imagine that if you meet a really humble man he will be what most people call "humble" nowadays: he will not be a sort of greasy, smarmy person, who is always telling you that, of course, he is nobody. Probably all you will think about him is that he seemed a cheerful, intelligent chap who took a real interest in what *you* said to *him*. If you do dislike him it will be because you feel a little envious of anyone who seems to enjoy life so easily. He will not be thinking about humility; he will not be thinking about himself at all.[15]

It should be considered crazy when we settle for the pseudo strength that comes from positional power and the command-and-control structures of human systems. We have the choice to lean into the power of Christ Jesus by picking up the servant's towel and joining the servant culture of the greatest Servant of all.

FIVE

THE SERVANTSHIP CULTURE
A FELLOWSHIP OF CO-LABORERS

On my male servants and female servants in those days I will pour out my Spirit.

—Acts 2:18

When we no longer see dominance and social influence as the basic activities of leadership, we no longer think of people in terms of leaders and followers. Instead, we can think of leadership as a process in which an entire community is engaged.

—Len Hjalmarson[1]

ld ways are like so many Bruce Willis action flicks. They die hard. We all have the habit of reverting to familiar methods of doing things. It seems that despite all the attention given to Bible reading, spiritual formation, and missional-hearted output, we still think of churches as organizations rather than the holistic, living, breathing, body of Christ. We have approached staffs in ministries and churches from the perspective of clock builders rather than community caretakers. Our incessant demands for prediction and control have been placed on the precious saints the apostle Paul called "yokefellow[s]" (Phil. 4:3, KJV). This is a term that speaks of marriage bonds, collegiality, camaraderie, and partnership. "Yokefellow" harkens to the tool used to join two oxen in unison. A yoke was a simple mechanism made from a pole with two side-by-side U-shaped devices that fit over the necks of the oxen. The word in the Greek means "to pull together in harness." To call someone your yokefellow is to say, "We are in this thing together, shoulder to shoulder. We may have differing strengths, but we are both just a couple of oxen whose reins are in the hands of the same Master."

One simple change of paradigm can alter our entire way of seeing things. When we view church as a business, we will undoubtedly treat those who should be our yokefellows and peers as employees and subordinates. This is not to say that everyone has the same role. Different giftings and talents equip us all for different roles. What causes us to go off the rails—through the sin of lording over others—is the tendency to rank the rarer gifts and talents of a few servants above the more common gifts and talents held by others. This is where a significant paradigm shift is needed for those with giftings from among the stronger five-fold areas of shepherd, teacher, evangelist, prophet, and apostle.

Here's the deal. No matter how rare your gifts are, you are not to treat anyone in the fellowship as *your* servant. Every individual in the body is a servant of the Lord. In fact, Jesus said if you want to be great, *you* are the one who must be the most fervent servant. You are nothing more than an ox, a beast of burden, yoked with another ox that may be less gifted in your area of strength. He or she is not behind you. He or she is shoulder to shoulder with you. Just as you have stronger giftings in certain areas, no doubt that same ox you are harnessed to has giftings and talents to which yours pale in comparison.

This is not to say that everyone has the same level of responsibility. We may be carrying more responsibility in certain areas than others. Some team members are assigned the task of assisting other, more seasoned or mature, servants. The message here is about attitude and posture. The "It shall not be so among you" dictum of Jesus means there is to be an upside-down difference in the way we relate to one another as we serve *him* together in *his* kingdom. The way we relate to one another should stand in stark contrast to the ways of the Gentiles.

These are among the reasons that Jesus doesn't want us calling ourselves leaders. Language matters big time and our choices of words shape the cultures of our churches and ministries. We must agree that Jesus could not have been clearer on these matters:

You all have a single Teacher, and you are all classmates. Don't set people up as experts over your life, letting them tell you what to do. Save that authority for God; let him tell you what to do. No one else should carry the title of "Father"; you have only one Father, and he's in heaven. And don't let people maneuver you into taking charge of them. There is only one Life-Leader for you and them—Christ.

Do you want to stand out? Then step down. Be a servant. (Matt. 23:8-11, TM)

BAD LANGUAGE

Jesus said to his disciples, "I have called you *friends*" (John 15:15, emphasis added). He didn't say, "I have called you employees." We should be asking ourselves, "If Jesus didn't do that, why do we?" It is not hard to determine whether a church or denominational culture is servant centric or employee centric; these are the tell-all facts of whether a ministry is operating as a faith community or as a business. Are staff members treated and spoken to in ways that volunteer church members would never be treated and spoken to? If the honest answer is yes, then your ministry is being run as a business and not as a community of faithful servants, yoked in a co-follower relationship. Are staffers or are staffers not members of that local church body, just like all of the nonvocational members? Wayne Alderson writes, "Workers know when they are being bought instead of valued. Being bought is an act that is conditional, manipulative, demanding, and rooted in a control mentality. It's the exact opposite of being valued."[2]

This may come as a shock, but the difference between a church staff and a business staff is that no one in a church should ever be viewed as or called an employee—and certainly not *your* employee. By what right or biblical concept does any senior or executive pastor have to say that another servant in the church is his or her employee? There is no biblical precedent for such thinking. In contemporary terms an employee is a hireling, a person who performs a job for money. The word "employee" is a business sector term; to call the servants in our churches, denominations, or any other ministries employees is to admit, "Yes, we view ourselves as a business and operate as one." Just pull out a *Webster's* dictionary and see for yourself: an employee is "a person hired by another, or by a business firm, . . . to work for wages or salary."[3]

This is not to say that all employees in businesses are just there for the money. Many people absolutely love their jobs. In fact, the word "vocation" gets its roots from the Latin word that means "calling." There are a myriad of people who, if you ask whether they like their jobs, will begin to gush about how much they love doing what they do. Sometimes people will remark that they can't believe they get paid to do what they do. The hope is that everyone would be able to find the true calling on his or her life and the joy that comes from serving from it.

Recognizing that hired workers in the business world are called employees, kingdom of God perspectives cannot be emphasized enough. The church has no employees. They are blessed to have servants of Christ whom the collective fellowship affirms as being sent by the Lord to serve as co-laborers. The fellowship supports them financially, just as they support overseas missionaries or people in a variety of ministries. But these people don't *work for* the church or any leader at the church. They *serve* the Lord and his people.

There is a major problem when we use boss-employee terminology in our church cultures, for that is to label servants of God as hirelings. There can be only one reason to do so—in order to establish command and control over others, using money as a ball and chain. Boss-employee language is used as a constant and clear reminder of who has the upper hand in the relationship. It also calls to mind the consequences for the lower-ranking individual who fails to stay put in his or her place. Let Jesus' words echo again, "It will not be so among you."

A CHURCH LEADERSHIP SCENARIO

Rob[4] is a friend who joined a church that was deeply involved in overseas missions. He is an incredibly driven and smart guy with a background in military Special Forces. He is also a triathlete. Rob is a quick learner and a go-getter. He began to join in on some trips to a few places where the church was working, eventually leading some initiatives in a region the church had not previously been. In short order Rob had pioneered the new ministry and had raised half of the necessary funds to leave his well-paying "real" job in order to serve the new mission full-time. The church matched the funds Rob had raised, freeing him to give all his attention to the new mission.

After a couple of years the ministry was flourishing and Rob was as well. Everyone agreed that he was doing a marvelous job. Then a problem arose. The senior pastor called Rob to tell him he had "great" news. The new budget included funds to pay Rob's entire salary so that he would no longer have to raise his own funds for the ministry. He could now be a full-time pastor on the church staff. The pastor was stunned when Rob cheerfully said, "That's great. I appreciate it. But use those funds for something else. I'm doing fine. The ministry over there is developing like crazy. What we are doing is working great. Let's just keep going as we have been."

Rob would have loved to have given up the task of personal fund-raising, but he had been around the culture of this church for too long. He was well aware that those who were full-time staff members were not allowed to self-manage and carry out their ministries and callings with the freedom he enjoyed. The culture of the church was extremely hierarchical and top down. My friend's instincts said the reason the senior pastor wanted to fund him fully was in order to *own* him as an employee. His instincts were right. A week later Rob was summoned to the senior pastor's office, where in a ten-minute meeting with the big guy and the executive pastor, he was told his ministry with the church was over. Yippee-ki-yay!

It is imperative that we embrace the paradigm of the kingdom of God as being phenomenally antithetical to the kingdoms of the world. It is within this kingdom—the domain of God—that the church is embedded. Our titles, language, relationships, and uses of power come from a totally different perspective than the kingdoms of humankind. Jesus didn't come to make a few adjustments. He came and turned the entire system on its head. To operate within our churches using practices and measures that so often contradict the ethics of the kingdom of God is to stand in opposition to the King of the kingdom. And to assume titles and positions he has reserved for himself could, and possibly should, be considered treacherous at best and treasonous at worst.

MUTUAL SUBMISSION

Be subject . . . to every fellow worker and laborer. (1 Cor. 16:16)

[Submit] to one another out of reverence for Christ. (Eph. 5:21)

It takes a ton of grace, patience, and humility to lay down one's opinions on the table of mutual submission. It also takes a ton of faith. But shouldn't faith define our churches? If we lay claim to the moniker of faith community, we are declaring to one another, and the watching world, that we are a community that lives by and through faith on every level. At the leadership level—which by now you know I am calling the servantship level—we must have faith in the presence and voice of God in others throughout the local church body.

My friend David Fitch is both a seminary professor and a church planter whose primary spiritual gift is apostolic. He has an infectious smile and a loving and caring heart, but he has strong opinions and is more than scholarly enough to make his stand theologically. To put it differently, David has a charismatic and powerful personality. He possesses the skill and natural ability to get his way—that is, if he were to choose to use power to do so.

For several years I have made a habit of reading David's blog (www.reclaimingthemission.com). Something I have noticed is that when he writes a particularly opinionated or controversial article, he invariably concludes it with phrases such as, "What do you think?" and "Am I right on this?" The question is never rhetorical. It is always asked in a genuinely humble manner, as in, "I know I have a strong view of this, but I could certainly be wrong and would love to hear your thoughts."

I have read a lot of David's thoughts about mutual submission as the process by which his church is led. One evening over dinner in Chicago I asked him to share with me how mutual submission works in his church. David began by saying that as a person with strong apostolic gifting he does in fact come up with a lot of ideas. He is a forward thinker with a heavy dose of entrepreneurial overtones. David said, "When I have an idea, concern, or opinion on an issue, I bring it to the other members of the team of fivefold [Eph. 4:11-12] elders and say, 'I have something I want to submit to you.'" At that point, David stopped and said, "Do you see that? I say, 'I want to *submit* this to you.'" David mentioned the use of submissive language to season the conversation in grace and humility and to emphasize the mutual submission he and the others were committed to. He then discussed how the idea he laid on the table would be handled.

If all the other elders are in agreement, the idea will then be submitted in prayer, set on the proverbial altar before the Lord for a time, and revisited to see if God had spoken anything different to any team members in the meantime. The same scenario is played out if there is disagreement from any or all of the other elders. The idea or issue is submitted to the Lord in prayer and revisited later. If there is still not complete agreement on how to move forward, the issue is left on the prayer altar indefinitely. David then grabbed a napkin and began to sketch out three points that he has subsequently blogged on:

1. *Posture*: Anyone in a recognized role of leadership is called to maintain the posture of submission to Jesus Christ as Lord of the church and to model the posture of mutual submission to all others who are in the sphere of leadership. It is from this position that one can expect to witness God's truth revealed for the fellowship. The dialogue emerging from sharing and listening, debating and praying, births consensus. Until consensus emerges, there is more waiting and listening.

2. *Process*: Jesus lays out a detailed process in Matt. 18 that provides fundamental steps for navigating disputable matters or issues that arise within the community of his followers. The binding and loosing terminology opens this process for application beyond sin issues between individuals. David writes,

> We go to one another and in humility discuss the issue. If we believe someone is in sin, we say that and

then submit ourselves to that person, being careful to listen as to why we might be wrong. If agreement cannot be reached, if insubordination is detected, we then bring in a third person. At the point where an issue simply cannot be agreed upon (and these issues are rare and outside the creedal orthodoxies that guide a given church), then we take it to the elders, then to the community to study and pray over the issue (Acts 15:28). The Holy Spirit at work in the community drives the issues that will determine the direction of the church, not the single chosen leader who shall determine what shall be discerned, what shall be tolerated, and what shall [not be] allowed."[5]

3. *Pneumatocracy*: Having its roots in the word *pneuma* (spirit), the idea of a Spirit-driven leadership certainly is what we all should be searching for. In terms of governance or leadership, the idea of pneumatocracy speaks of a collective voice derived from apostles, prophets, teachers, evangelists, and pastors who are recognized by the faith community. "Each one must be given authority for what gifts God has given them. Yet they must exercise that gift in grace and humility (Rom 12:3-4)."[6]

Undoubtedly many who read this will wonder what happens when we face a pressing issue that demands an immediate decision. What if a fork in the road occurs and a directional decision must be made? Coming into agreement is hard work and *heart* work. If you have ever been married, you know how true that is. We find no particular model or script in the New Testament that gives us a definitive model or prescription for how to make decisions, which is one of the big leadership issues we wrestle with. What we do have is clarity on the attitude and persona we are to possess along the way. This has to do with the tone and tenor of how our leadership must be carried out and manifested in our churches. The fruit of the Spirit and the character and persona of Jesus are not foggy. What we *can* see and hear clearly from reading the New Testament are some of the ways with which we are instructed *not* to operate and the ethos with which we are always to interact with one another.

PLURALITY OF OVERSIGHT

No pattern can be found of a *single-decider* leadership ethos in the accounts of the churches in the New Testament. The notion of a single leader overseeing a church has no foundation in the New Testament. *Shared* oversight is what we find in the pages of our Bibles. The following citations all speak to plurality of oversight in the churches:

- The church in Jerusalem—Acts 11:30
- The churches in Galatia—Acts 14:23
- The church in Ephesus—Acts 20:17
- The church in Philippi—Phil. 1:1
- The churches in Judea—James 5:14
- The churches in Crete—Titus 1:5

What is missing in these passages and the entire New Testament is any intimation whatsoever of senior pastors, chief among equals, or one-man-rule/the-buck-stops-here leaders. The proverbial "buck" stops at the feet of the Holy Spirit, who resides in those he calls as a collective body of wisdom. It is through this collective body that the Holy Spirit alone is Chief Counselor. The biblical account is one of elders who relied on the voice of the Holy Spirit and who stood on equal footing with each other. There is no doubt that they exercised different types of giftings, but there is no hint of a vertical manager-worker, rank-and-file structure. Throughout the book of Acts different men, such as Peter and James, functioned as spokesmen on certain occasions, but not one of them occupied a permanent seat of authority over the others. In his book *Reimagining Church*, Frank Viola writes,

> Consequently, the modern offices of "senior pastor," "chief elder," and "head pastor" simply did not exist in the early church. The first-century Christians didn't mark off one man among the college of elders and elevate him to a superior position of authority. The elders were not part of a

chain of command that put them under Christ and over the church. They weren't part of a hierarchical pyramid. They were simply members of the body of Christ, not an elite oligarchy.[7]

The Lord initiated a relational system that enables us to be disentangled from fleshly power and authority systems and structures of leadership. It is called the household of God.

FAMILY AFFAIR

The idea of family was the image and language Jesus used as he was building his band of followers into what would become the church. He was not giving the church a social strategy. The church was and is to *be* a social strategy. To adopt the mechanics and processes of the fallen world is to cheapen and degrade the glorious family of God, which should be one of the most attractive features to a watching world. The familial language that saturates the Gospels and the New Testament Epistles underscores an ethos of the church as family. It is not an organization, and it is only an institution as it is the institution of a family.

In the light of this, we should consider it ludicrous to approach the development of our local churches from the perspective of managers and administrative leadership. We should detest such a notion that robs us of life and genuine relationship. Who would want to get up in the morning to work at a corporation when they could join the family around the breakfast table in sweet communion and true fellowship? Jesus' statements about the position of the Father are very telling for the function of the church as a family. In Matt. 23:9 he commands his followers to "call no man your father on earth, for you have one Father, who is in heaven." In another passage, more subtly, Jesus reserves the position of patriarch in the family of God for the heavenly Father alone:

Peter began to say to him, "See, we have left everything and followed you." Jesus said, "Truly, I say to you, there is no one who has left house or brothers or sisters or mother or father or children or lands, for my sake and for the gospel, who will not receive a hundredfold now in this time, houses and brothers and sisters and mothers and children and lands, with persecutions, and in the age to come eternal life." (Mark 10:28-30)

Jesus acknowledges that he is aware that natural relationships are sometimes abandoned in various degrees when a person begins to follow him. He then says that anyone who has left brothers, sisters, mother, father, or children will receive a hundredfold return in brothers, sisters, mothers, and children.

Notice what is missing? Answer: fathers. Jesus emphasizes that the church is a family, a huge family, in fact—with many siblings, mothers, and children—but it is a one-father family and God is that father. We don't receive many fathers. Jesus wants us to be clear that God is the Leader in the community. From the book of Acts forward, the New Testament is soaked in familial language. The words "brother" and "sister" are used in excess of 250 times in the context of church-family relationships. As pointed out earlier, language plays an enormous role in the shaping of cultures. The Holy Spirit-inspired writers of the New Testament did not use familial language to the extent they did by accident.

In her book *Followership* Barbara Kellerman provides insight into the latest studies and new science of siblings that underscores the underappreciated influence of sibling relationships:

By the time children are eleven years old, they spend approximately 33 percent of their free time with their siblings, more than they spend with their parents, teachers, friends, or even by themselves. In fact, from the time they are born, our brothers and sisters are our collaborators and co-conspirators, our role models and cautionary tales. What we can say, then, is that followers follow each other first and foremost because they model their behavior on others similar to themselves. Followers also follow other followers for some of the same reasons they follow their leaders. That is, followers go along with other followers because they (1) lend stability and security, (2) provide order and meaning, and (3) constitute the group to which they want to belong. Of course, when followers follow other followers, as opposed to following their leaders, formal rank plays little or even no meaningful role. No one is designated superior—which means no one is the designated subordinate. We see this in informal groups, such as children together in a playground.[8]

I find that last sentence to be wonderfully intriguing in the light of Jesus' emphasis for us to become like children in order to enter the kingdom of God. We need to lighten up and just let the life of God flow through us. Children have the ability to self-organize enough to make the game work just fine without getting uptight about it.

Who doesn't love a great mystery? Answer: church leaders. We need to rediscover the great mystery that is part of walking with another as we walk with God. It is one of the joys of being with Jesus. Can you imagine what it must of have been like on a "normal" day for the original twelve disciples? Every day those guys must have jumped out of bed, thinking, "I can't wait to see what he has up his sleeve for us today!" That dream is lost on almost all clergy.

The overwrought leadership constructs that we looked at in the first part of this book actually seek to eliminate almost all the mystery attached to journeying with God. Even our worship services are dictated to the very minute of what will happen next. There is virtually no opportunity for the Holy Spirit to lead most contemporary church worship services once they begin. But servantship takes us to the place where we are hanging on for the ride of a lifetime. Jesus said we must assume the posture of a little child if we hope to enter into the joys waiting for us in the kingdom of God. And we get to do so with our brothers and sisters.

CULTURES OF TRUST

Anyone who commits himself or herself to developing a servantship community must embrace the concept of living systems, with communication habits generated and sustained by relationships. Servantship cultures are atmospheres where information flows freely. Leadership-centric cultures typically are not this way. Information is disseminated on a need-to-know basis, according to the hierarchical chart. For a living system such as a church—the body of Christ—when information stops formation stops (i.e., "in" + "formation"). And when formation ceases, *real* growth ceases. Just because a body is getting big doesn't mean it is alive. I spent a lot of my youth fishing and hunting on land owned by cattlemen. From time to time I would come across a dead cow, whose carcass was inflated with intestinal gasses. That taught me that even dead bodies can get bloated, appearing to be growing, but just full of hot air.

Truth systems are open systems. But many denominations and churches have leadership cultures of fear. The top-down leadership hierarchy of command and control is so entrenched that invisible boundaries—walls of fear and mistrust—determine the degree of honest exchange among staff members. In many of these ministries staff members would never consider having a sincere and completely honest discussion with the senior pastor or an executive leader within the church or denomination for fear of reprisal.

Two former church staff members I interviewed (from different churches) shared their personal accounts of opening up to another staff member about their feelings of a possible change coming in their lives. It was a change that could include serving in another ministry. They didn't know where or when but just sensed a change *might* be coming. In both instances an upper-echelon leader got word of the conversation, called the staff member in, and immediately sent the person packing for lack of loyalty and for "obviously" not being committed to the church and its vision. Can you hear the echo? "It will not be so among you."

Wherever you encounter an atmosphere of fear, you can be sure you have walked into a culture of command and control. The ones in control are afraid of not being in control, and they parlay their own fear into tools of control over others. The leadership moxie is so strong that staff members who are not classified as "senior" or "executive" exist not as *called* ones but as *hired* ones. And anyone who has been hired knows he or she can just as easily be fired.

Truth is never the strong suit in cultures of fear—pretense is. Where systems of fear and control exist, truth is limited and, to a larger degree, shut down. People are afraid to share their honest opinions, concerns, and even creative ideas. It is too dangerous to take the chance of being honest with opinions and feelings. It naturally follows that Jesus does not show up because God does not give a spirit of fear, much less lead with one. Churches and ministries that have cultures such as these must rely more and more on fleshly techniques because they have less and less of the Holy Spirit to draw from. These groups are cultivated in fear, not in the love of Christ: "There is no room in love for fear. Well-formed love banishes fear. Since fear is crippling, a fearful life—fear of death, fear of judgment—is one not yet fully formed in love" (1 John 4:18, TM).

Organizational behavior expert Margaret Wheatley says, "In classical thermodynamics, equilibrium is the end state in the evolution of closed systems, the point at which the system has exhausted all of its capacity for change, done its work, and dissipated its productive capacity into entropy."[9] When entropy begins, it means that movement has ceased. The free exchange of ideas is shut down, and change has no chance of taking place. This is a warning sign of impending death.

Hierarchy and titles are inferior substitutes for servantship cultures. They are incompatible with genuine community. Playing the rank card bypasses the time and energy required to marinate in relationship, with the chaos of fair fighting; wrestling; dealing with our own egos, preferences, and ideas; and downright demanding our own way. Peter Senge, whose best-selling book *The Fifth Discipline* is on the shelves of thousands of evangelical leaders, shares,

> In the knowledge era, we will finally have to surrender the myth of leaders as isolated heroes commanding their organizations from on high. Top-down directives, even when they are implemented, reinforce an environment of fear, distrust, and internal competitiveness that reduces collaboration and cooperation. They foster compliance instead of commitment, yet only genuine commitment can bring about the courage, imagination, patience, and perseverance necessary in a knowledge-creating organization. For those reasons, leadership in the future will be distributed among diverse individuals and teams who share responsibility for creating the organization's future.[10]

The price we pay for closed systems is the loss of the God-given impartation and gift bounty that "lower-rung" servants can bring—if only they were allowed to. How often we must miss out on holy gems and divine words from the Lord through "employees" because they are muted by the remote control of church bosses. Closed systems seek equilibrium, and they get it. We talk about the need for balance. Balance is good for propellers or wheels that draw their power from motors or downward slopes. But balance will stop the movement of anything linear. Our fascination with equilibrium has come at the expense of the holistic processes that develop and sustain ongoing life— real life. Equilibrium stops movement, and when it reigns in our churches, we will never see a missional movement blossom. The God-gifted servants are institutionalized, and their dreams and missional imaginations are constrained in the handcuffs and leg-irons of command-and-control church bosses.

ENCOURAGING SELF-MANAGEMENT

A few years ago I served at a megachurch with an executive pastor whose previous experience was exclusively within the corporate business sector. There were a couple of other guys that served in my area, and we began to spend the first twenty to thirty minutes of our day in worship and prayer together. I would grab my guitar, and we would just tune our hearts together in communion with one another and the Lord. It was quickly becoming a deeply enriching and energizing way to begin our day as a ministry team. We each practiced a rhythm of personal devotion at our homes earlier in the morning, but this was on top of that. After about two weeks of our morning worship times, word got around to the executive pastor, who informed us that we were not to be doing this on "work time." If we wanted to continue to do so, that was fine, but we would need to come in earlier and do it on our "own" time. If he had been totally honest, the executive pastor would have said, "Tell Jesus you are not to be wasting your time with him on the church's dollar."

It is important to understand the scenario and context of this incident because the role of executive pastor has become a trend over the last few years, and not all but many of the people who work in these roles are similar to the guy in this story. Their experience is from the business sector, and they are given authority and final say over men and women who have been serving in vocational ministry for years and years. In this case, between myself and my other two friends there was almost fifty years of ministerial and pastoral experience represented. Nonetheless, the hierarchical system dictated ways and means, regardless of outcomes. The executive pastor never once suggested that we were not accomplishing our goals and tasks. All three of us were leading ministries that were flourishing. In other words—we were getting our job done.

The role of executive pastor, with this type of domineering authority, is a surging trend across the landscape of the evangelical church world. I have never quite understood micromanagers. It seems reasonable that if someone does not trust the person he or she hired or chose to handle a particular task or area of responsibility, then it is a reflection on his or her own poor judgment for choosing that person in the first place. In ministry settings it goes further. In church circles I want to ask those who demand to manage their fellow servants, "Do you or do you not trust the presence of the Holy Spirit and the pouring out of the gifts of Jesus on the person tasked with responsibilities to carry out those responsibilities?" Hear the words of the apostle:

> I therefore, a prisoner for the Lord, urge you to walk in a manner worthy of the calling to which you have been called, with all humility and gentleness, with patience, bearing with one another in love, eager to maintain the unity of the Spirit in the bond of peace. There is one body and one Spirit—just as you were called to the one hope that belongs to your call—one Lord, one faith, one baptism, one God and Father of all, who is over all and through all and in all. But grace was given to each one of us according to the measure of Christ's gift. Therefore it says, "When he ascended on high he led a host of captives, and he gave gifts to men." (Eph. 4:1-8)

This passage is not just about the general unity of the body of Christ. Paul could have simply said, "Everybody, get along!" But he brings up the gifting thing. Paul points out the diversity of the body that is manifest in the differing gifts that Jesus himself has poured out on each body member. He implores everyone to walk in humility, patience, and love as those gifts manifest among one another. Paul then carries the thought further, pointing out the importance of this for developing a mature body of believers:

> And he gave the apostles, the prophets, the evangelists, the shepherds and teachers, to equip the saints for the work of ministry, for building up the body of Christ, until we all attain to the unity of the faith and of the knowledge of the Son of God, to mature manhood, to the measure of the stature of the fullness of Christ, so that we may no longer be children, tossed to and fro by the waves and carried about by every wind of doctrine, by human cunning, by craftiness in deceitful schemes. (Vv. 11-14)

Self-management is not about creating a Wild West, renegade, free-for-all culture where accountability is nonexistent. It is about the collective servantship community that affirms Christ has distributed particular gifts to certain men and women. And those people are to be released and trusted to exercise their gifts for the sake of the overall body of believers. Yes, they are to give account for the results of their stewardship of responsibilities, finances, and the like—while maintaining a posture of mutual submission to the overall community. They are to give an account of how they are using the collective resources of the church or ministry body. But people should be trusted, not bossed or managed. They are accountable to the entire community, not one or two people who occupy positions of hierarchy over the rest of the community of co-followers. Again, no such arrangement, model, or pattern can be found anywhere in the New Testament churches.

The passages above are to be applied to the interactive relational dynamics of church staffs. Where did we get the wrongheaded notion that these scriptures don't apply to the working relationships of our church staffs? Where did we get the idea of "firing" people who have been called to serve vocationally in our churches? Why would we assume that the Matt. 18 process of settling issues and disputes between believers does not apply to our church staffs? Do you hear the echo? "It will not be so among you."

If there was ever a place where we need to apply scriptural direction with as much vigor as possible, you would think it would be on our church staffs. Why in the world would we feel the need to look to business sector gurus for human-resource advice when the Lord of the church has given us an entire manuscript on how to proceed? Churches across the Western world are cluttered with command-and-control policies and procedures that strangle the life from the body of Christ because they jettison the New Testament when it comes to inner-office procedures. These are devices born from fear, and they create and perpetrate cultures of fear.

Our imaginations need to be recaptured by the idea of Jesus and *his* church. He said, "I will build my church, and the gates of hell shall not prevail against it" (Matt. 16:18). The two key words in that emphatic statement are "I" and "my." Jesus is both the Builder and owner of the church. He is very much capable of building his own church without our help. Our only job is to *be* the church. The church is a living system with the innate ability to self-organize for sustainability and growth.

In *The Forgotten Ways,* a book that has become a seminal volume of missiology across the world, Alan Hirsch wrote about the astonishing growth of the Chinese church following the edicts and persecution precipitated by Mao Tse-tung, whose purge of religion through the banishment of missionaries and murder of ministers and church leaders aimed at obliterating Christianity from China:

> At the end of the reign of Mao and his system in the late seventies, and the subsequent lifting of the so-called Bamboo Curtain in the early eighties, foreign missionaries and church officials were allowed back into the country, albeit under strict supervision. They expected to find the church decimated and the disciples a weak and battered people. On the contrary, they discovered that Christianity had flourished beyond all imagination. The estimates then were about 60 million Christians in China and counting! And it has grown significantly since then. If anything, in the Chinese phenomenon we are witnessing the most significant transformational Christian movement in the history of the church.[11]

Understand, the Chinese Christians had no professional clergy, no policies and procedures, no structure of leadership, and no central office issuing orders down lines of authority. Yet they grew like mad. And they continue to grow today. The Chinese Christians have done it by *the* book—the Bible. They have taken the biblical approach of believing that Jesus can and will build his church. Servantship communities are developed as cultures of true partnership and commonality at all levels. The ownership of the mission goes further than merely participating or contributing with minimal input. Co-laboring servants take the initiative and summon the courage to assume these responsibilities:

- Personal care and growth (ongoing education, spiritual formation, health)
- Self-awareness and assessment
- Personal motivation
- Taking initiative
- Shaping the culture of the group
- Rewriting the "rules" when useful
- Improving processes
- Completing tasks
- Offering feedback

Those are signposts of a culture built on freedom, mutual respect, and trust. It is a family fellowship—a culture that treats people like actual adults.

One of the most important breakthroughs of quantum physics lies in understanding a world in which the only material form is that of relationships. No individual exists independent of relationships. At the human level, all groups and organizations must be viewed as webs of relationships. The big shift comes in realizing that control and order are not synonymous. Believe it or not, you *can* have order without control. One of the least intelligent things an organization or leader can do is to assume the people God has called there have no real intelligence themselves. The Jesus-style servantship culture is almost completely sociologically antithetical to the "Gentile" leadership culture. Amazingly, several cultural anthropologists are coming to many of the same conclusions. Peter Block, a profound thinker on the social dynamics of community, writes, "Community transformation calls for citizenship that shifts the context from a place of fear and fault, law and oversight, corporation and "systems," and preoccupation with leadership to one of gifts, generosity, abundance; social fabric and chosen accountability; and associational life and the engagement of citizens."[12]

CONGREGATION OR COMMUNITY?

The church growth era served us well for reimagining evangelism and the church as an inviting place for the unchurched. It spun off the seeker church movement that brought a key element back into focus. We should be thankful for voices such as Bill Hybels and Rick Warren, who have played key roles in turning the eyes and hearts of evangelical leaders toward those outside the church. But the caveat of the seeker movement was that it labeled the unchurched person as the seeker, while Jesus portrayed himself as the Seeker in Luke 15. While owing much to the seeker movement for its renewal of the evangelistic ethos for the church, the present-day missional movement has stepped up to reorient the perspective of the saints to see themselves as the seekers.

The concern is that the seeker church movement places incredibly high value and focus on church as an event. A prevailing amount of energy, resource, imagination, and promotion goes toward presenting a weekly service whereby church members are encouraged to bring their unchurched friends in order to be influenced with a positive message tied to the Bible. This has produced several unintended results. We will briefly look at two of them.

First, the primary role of the saints (a.k.a. church members) is to support the staff in creating and presenting the weekend event, called a church service. Church members are encouraged to invite friends to the services and to support the church service by taking roles as ushers, greeters, singers, actors, stagehands, children's workers, and so on. Again, this book is not about how to formulate church services, so I am not going there. The issue here is that very often in seeker churches, church members' spiritual gifts (Rom. 12; 1 Cor. 12; Eph. 4) are almost completely ignored. The spiritual gifts are compartmentalized and reserved as categories for clergy (paid staff) only. This promotes the fallacy of a clergy-laity divide—a crippling and heretical perspective of the body of Christ.

Second, most of the church members assume the role of a passive audience rather than an actual connected assembly of believers. We end up with a congregation but not a community. The saints sit on the planks once a week and never mix their lives together. Church members are convinced that *real* church consists of the stable, predictable congregating of fellow believers for an hour or so each week.

Congregations	Communities
• Are like restaurants	• Are like culinary art schools
• Observe	• Participate
• Need architects	• Need gardeners
• Are collected	• Are connected

OVER AND UNDER

The corporate business sector, which operates with charts, ladders of status, and rank, is hypnotized by visions of hierarchy. The concept of level after level of subordinates is engrained in the systemic makeup of almost every company. Looking at military branches we see clear distinctions of ranks. There is no question or guessing needed to determine who is over whom. For those of us in the church, our reality is that there is only one superior-subordinate relationship. Jesus is the one and only Superior. He is our one ranking Officer. Every one of us is a subordinate.

Working relationships within the servantship culture of the church are to be carried out through willing submission to one another. Each member is gifted by Christ and the Holy Spirit with differing degrees and strengths of spiritual gifts. The members (people) that make up the body of Christ are each under the headship and rule of Jesus. There are distinctions of responsibility, but they are not to be subjugated to the command and control of a human hierarchy. They are carried out through a relational web of mutual submission and accountability, held in check—not by human dictate—but by obedience to Scripture and under the influence of the Holy Spirit.

Hear the words of Paul, speaking to the relational nature of the gifted saints, working together in mutual submission: "Rather, speaking the truth in love, we are to grow up in every way into him who is the head, into Christ, from whom the whole body, joined and held together by every joint with which it is equipped, when each part is working properly, makes the body grow so that it builds itself up in love" (Eph. 4:15-16).

Notice the phrase "the whole body, joined and held together by every joint with which it is equipped" (v. 16). The body of Christ holds itself together by the equipping hand of Jesus. Paul then says, "When each part is working properly, [Christ] makes the body grow so that it *builds itself* up in love" (v. 16, emphasis added). Paul declares that the body of Christ is sufficiently equipped to hold itself together and to build itself up, based on its mutual submission to one another, under the headship of Jesus. The failure to embrace this way of body life and leadership is the cause of so much pastoral burnout. No one person is called or designed to carry the weight and responsibility for a church.

I am convinced that the present-day weakness in the body of Christ in the West is tied directly to leadership systems that dominate our churches. The body is weak because it is not allowed to function as Paul said it should. Each part of the body is *not* "working properly." The body is not allowed to build "itself up in love." It is held down by the power and control of a hierarchical few who believe they are the only competent ones to run it.

When our heart (member) is working in coordination with our lungs (member), our kidneys (member), and the other organs (members), and our hands (member) are feeding our mouth (member) and so on, life and growth happen. The collective intelligence of the body is present in sufficient measure to generate growth and edification of itself. The body grows, not because someone pushes it to grow, but because it contains the necessary ingredients to do so through the relationship of each connected member. It is a beautifully mystical thing. But humans can never manufacture such life.

The church is referred to as the *body* of Christ because it is exactly that. It is a living system. Margaret Wheatley speaks of the ability of living systems to function through *autopoiesis*, a word from Greek, which means "self-producing" or "self-making." She writes,

Autopoiesis is life's fundamental process for creating and renewing itself, for growth and change. A living system is a network of processes in which every process contributes to all other processes. The entire network is engaged together in producing itself. Each organism maintains a clear sense of its individual identity within a larger network of relationships that helps shape its identity. Each being is noticeable as a separate entity, yet it is simultaneously part of a whole system.[13]

As with autopoiesis, leadership processed as mutually submissive servantship places tremendous faith in the Lord, working his wisdom, ways, and means throughout the entire body. The fallacy of the modern leadership culture is that it is shaped and drawn from the modern world of engineering and mechanics. The assumption is that people must be managed and maintained just as you would a machine. We assume that, just like a machine, the worker has no desire, no heart, no feeling, no passion, and no significant intelligence to speak of. After all, machines have none of that.

For life to exist in a body it must be allowed to create and participate in its own development and reason for existing. As co-followers—servants and siblings in the family of God—we must not only trust each other to participate in the life of God together but also rejoice in the beauty of one another's creative, God-given graces. Who wants to see every artist work with the same medium or style? It is the diversity of styles that makes for a great gallery. So what if *I* wouldn't have done it *that* way? Good. Is the task getting completed? That is what matters. The self-organizing ability of the body of Christ—a living system—breeds shared understanding about what really matters. People can and will develop good and sufficient channels of communication when the atmosphere is conducive and encouraging.

OPEN AND BROKEN

The servantship culture is one of openness, authenticity, and permission for brokenness. It is anything but a "got it all together" culture. Mike Yaconelli, one of the founders of Youth Specialties, wrote of a dark time in his life when he took a pilgrimage to the L'Arche community where the renowned Henri Nouwen served the mentally and physically challenged:

Finally I accepted my brokenness. . . . I knew I was broken. I knew I was a sinner. I knew I continually disappointed God, but I could never accept that part of me. It was a part of me that embarrassed me. I continually felt the need to apologize, to run from my weaknesses, to deny who I was and concentrate on who I should be. I was broken, yes, but I was continually trying to never be broken again—or at least get to the place where I was very seldom broken.

At L'Arche, it became very clear to me that I had totally misunderstood the Christian faith. I came to see that it was in my brokenness, in my powerlessness, in my weakness that Jesus was made strong. It was in the acceptance of my lack of faith that God could give me faith. It was in the embracing of my brokenness that I could identify with others' brokenness. It was my role to identify with others' pain, not relieve it. Ministry was sharing, not dominating; understanding, not theologizing; caring, not fixing.[14]

The church is at her faithful best when she functions as a collective body of servants, allowing each and every member to contribute to the degree of his or her ability. Church staffs are at their trusting and performing best when their members allow one another to *be* the body of Christ rather than forcing some members to work as hired ones. The DNA of the life of Christ is more than enough within every local body of believers to shine the light of God's love to the watching world.

SIX

WHEN SERVANTS LEAD
REIMAGINING AUTHORITY

The human spirit was made to explore and soar, not to be regulated and intimidated. People are created to be free, not controlled; to experiment and make mistakes, not to be oiled and greased; to test their creative genes in order to reach their God-given potential, not to perform like machines or robots.

—Bill Easum[1]

The true kingdom of God is revolutionary. It is countercultural. It is upside-down from what we normally expect. Jesus is introducing a whole new form of governance. It is not a new idea for Jesus, but it is for us.

—Neil Cole[2]

n this top-down world of power and control, of haves and have-nots, it is especially difficult to get our minds around the idea of servantship as a realistic alternative to the vertical philosophy of leadership. The idea of handling authority in any way other than command and control is so very counterintuitive that it seems impossible. Couple this with a celebrity leadership culture that permeates Christianity through and through, and it is even harder to turn the gaze of ambitious young men and women away from aspirations of becoming the next church leadership star. It is a paradox that is quite perplexing and mind numbing. How is it possible to exercise authority that is as non-authoritarian as that conceived in the images of servantship? The answer comes when we derive authority in a way totally different from the domineering ways of a fallen world.

Across every sphere of life we encounter authority.[3] It is impossible to escape it, and we would be foolish to want to. To live in this fallen world without the oversight and supporting structures of law and order would be certain anarchy. Men and women who uphold statutes and laws are in place to govern a society whose members are not all godly. Law enforcers exercise their authority when facing resistance by using command-and-control methods, sometimes violently.

Every church mentioned in the New Testament also had authority. The apostle Paul made sure of it. But the authority in the world and the authority in the church are as different as life on two different planets. To understand authority in the church you must start from scratch in your thinking. You must toss out everything you've learned in this world about how authority is measured and practiced.

Jesus submitted to civil authority. He paid his taxes and never instigated civil insurrection. But he took the religious leaders to task when it came to the use of authority. As we have already observed, Jesus disallowed titles and hierarchy in the way he defined authority and its use for his followers. The government of his church sits on his shoulders and no one else's:

> For to us a child is born, to us a son is given; and the government shall be upon his shoulder, and his name shall be called Wonderful Counselor, Mighty God, Everlasting Father, Prince of Peace. Of the increase of his government and of peace there will be no end, on the throne of David and over his kingdom, to establish it and to uphold it with justice and with righteousness from this time forth and forevermore. The zeal of the Lord of hosts will do this. (Isa. 9:6-7)

Jesus was extensively clear about hierarchy. He could not have spelled it out any plainer. People get real nervous when anything but a vertical leadership chart is suggested. Why do we believe that Jesus can't be trusted to lead his own church? This is no doubt due in huge measure to what we have been taught all our lives compounded with all the books and conferences on leadership by best-selling Christian authors and megachurch pastors. Added to this mix is a daily sprinkling of tweets and social network posts containing assorted nuggets of wisdom on leadership.

WHAT ABOUT SUBMISSION?

Submission can be seen throughout the New Testament. Jesus modeled the epitome of submission in his relationship to the heavenly Father. And we have a multitude of examples throughout the Epistles that command people in all types of relationships to maintain submissive attitudes. From slaves to children, from young believers to ordinary citizens, the concept of submission is heavily themed across the pages of the New Testament. The biblical idea of submission is in no way being challenged or denied in this book. What must be challenged are the worldly ideas of submission and authority that have made their way into the church. Len Hjalmarson writes,

> The modern leader was the CEO, the manager of people and systems. Larry Crabb, in "The Safest Place on Earth," comments that we have a choice: we can be either managers

or mystics. Most of us feel somewhat out of place in community: we don't always feel safe and community itself is a mystery. We prefer structures we can understand and control. The problem is, God is less interested in predictability and control than we are! Or, from another perspective, He wants to be the one in control, and He doesn't always tell us in advance what He is up to! Or yet again, He may be more interested in the process than the goal; as leaders, we get fixated on goals because our identity is generally tied up in a particular view of success.[4]

Paul chose his words carefully as he wrote his epistles under the influence of the Holy Spirit. The words in this passage send a strong message of deep love and tender care and concern: "We ask you, brothers, to respect those who labor among you and are over you in the Lord and admonish you" (1 Thess. 5:12).

Let's unpack this verse, looking closer at three key phrases that relate to our current topic:

Respect *those . . .*

The word "respect" is a very poor translation. The King James Version actually gets it right, translating the word as "know." The Greek word *eidenai* means "to see" and "to know." It means to both perceive and experience something or someone by visiting with him or her. I have conversed with former staff members of some of the largest churches in America, persons who were in leadership positions of major departments or ministries. They have told me that throughout their many years of church service they never once had a one-on-one conversation with the senior pastor. When our churches are too big for team members to spend genuine time with one another, *knowing* one another, then maybe (probably) our churches have gotten too big.

Who labor **among** *you . . .*

What an interesting phrase. The word translated "among" means "to be beside" or "to be with." This speaks of position. If elders, deacons, or fivefold (Eph. 4:11-12) people with strong giftings are looking for their position—this is it. No one is to have position over another brother or sister in the servantship culture of the church. And this is where everything usually gets so skewed. We have built leadership structures that have created positions that set some people above—rather than among—others. I'm over you and you answer to me. You are to do what I tell you. When this structure exists, you can forget about fellowship and a functional family of God. Mutual submission gets nothing more than a wink and a nod.

*And are **over you** . . .*

"Over you" comes from a Greek word that means "protector" or "guardian." In no way does this word intimate positional, directive authority or supervision. It speaks to a function or role. Again, the idea of "among" conveys equality, while the idea of "over you" conveys loving and watchful care. We will dive deeper into this idea later in this chapter.

Admonish . . .

This is a word that simply means "to warn" or "to exhort." It carries a double meaning and responsibility. First, it is the responsibility to give a warning of impending danger to someone who is headed in a wrong direction. It is one of the most loving acts a person can perform, to warn another person who is going down a path beset with hidden pits or enemies preparing to ambush. Second, "admonish" carries with it the responsibility to encourage and build up. That is what it means to exhort—to build up. Nothing can substitute for having someone come alongside you with an encouraging word when you have failed or been let down in some way. It fills you with hope and confidence to get back on your horse and ride again.

In his first epistle, Peter writes something very similar to what Paul wrote to the Thessalonians: "The elders who are among you I exhort, I who am a fellow elder and a witness of the sufferings of Christ, and also a partaker of the glory that will be revealed: Shepherd the flock of God which is among you, serving as overseers, not by compulsion but willingly, not for dishonest gain but eagerly; nor as being lords over those entrusted to you, but being examples to the flock" (5:1-3, NKJV).

1. Peter speaks to the elders who are "among" the saints (v. 1, NKJV). This is their position. They are co-laborers, fellow servants, brothers and sisters.

2. He then says it again: "Shepherd [feed and care for] the flock of God that is *among* you" (v. 2, NKJV, emphasis added).

3. Next, he echoes the words of Paul: "serving as overseers" (v. 2, NKJV). The elders are exhorted to watch over—to oversee—the flock.

4. He exhorts them to do so "not by compulsion" or for money, which would make them hirelings, but out of service to the Lord (v. 2, NKJV).

5. Peter draws from his memory of walking with Jesus. How could he forget the day Jesus took the disciples to the woodshed concerning their desire for hierarchical position and the use of authority over others? "Jesus called them to him and said, 'You know that the rulers of the Gentiles *lord it over* them, and their great ones *exercise authority over* them'" (Matt. 20:25, emphasis added).

Peter tells the elders to carry out their oversight, not "as being *lords over* those entrusted to you" (1 Pet. 5:3, NKJV, emphasis added). Behaving as lords over others is an extremely dangerous thing to do. It is insidious at the core. It is even possibly demonic, because it comes close to assuming the position of God in someone's life. The title "lord" is reserved for Christ alone. To dominate others by use of our positions as elders, pastors, and so on, is incredibly dangerous territory to wander into. The scary thing is that many leaders in the church today don't wander into it; they run in and set up a throne.

Peter tags the sentence in verse 3 with the phrase "but being examples to the flock" (NKJV). He has now made the point that to lead in the kingdom of God is not to wield power and authority but to give loving oversight and, most of all, to be an example for others.

THE SENIOR PASTOR

At a seminar I recently spoke at for pastors and ministry leaders was a Hispanic brother who, during introductions, referred to himself as the associate pastor at so-and-so church. One of the guys at my table leaned over and said, "He's the senior pastor. But he won't call himself that. He says that Jesus is the Senior Pastor at his church. He even has it on his card. His title is associate pastor." This was serious business for this humble man. He understood something that few others do: "And when the Chief Shepherd appears, you will receive the crown of glory that does not fade away" (1 Pet. 5:4, NKJV).

Anyone who looks for the verses on *sola pastor* will get frustrated from flipping Bible pages. He or she will get just as frustrated searching for the positions of head pastor or senior pastor. The idea of senior or lead pastor is foreign to the New Testament. The concept is patently nonexistent. Maybe I should take that back. The idea does appear one time. As the quotation above indicates, Peter encourages elders to perform their functions in a way that will please the "Chief Shepherd" (v. 4, NKJV). His choice of the word *archipoimēn* is a Greek word constructed from the compound of *archi*, which means "ruler," and *poimēn*, which means "shepherd." There is a similar usage of *archi* in Acts 18:8, where the *archisynagōgos*, or "ruler of the synagogue," is mentioned.

Jesus is the one and only Chief, or Senior Pastor, found in the Bible. Of course, this title and position is not hard to find outside the Bible. Almost every evangelical church has a senior pastor. Such a position is a patent disregard of what Jesus forbade over and over. There is only one reason to hold on to such positions and titles—to reinforce and maintain hierarchies. They let everyone know who is in charge.

In recent years the concept of senior pastor has become so ingrained in evangelical churches that it has yielded a second-chair spin-off. Usually titled "executive pastor," this position joins the senior pastor to form a dynamic duo atop the local church leadership hierarchy. In the opening words of their book

Leading from the Second Chair, Bonem and Patterson set the stage for the top-down ideology that is so prevalent across the evangelical church landscape today:

> We have been frequent consumers of books, tapes, and conferences as a means of improving our leadership. Yet we have often felt frustration or discouragement after using these resources because they were not aimed at us. Their focus was the senior leader of the organization, the person who has the freedom and relative autonomy that comes with this top position. In the second chair, the amount of change you can initiate is limited because you are not the vision caster, the lead leader.
>
> . . . You do not have to be the number two person in an organizational hierarchy to be a second chair leader. In fact, our definition can include anyone who is not the lead leader. Every organization has a perceived pecking order.[5]

There is no nuance of top-down language here. Phrases such as "senior leader," "top position," "lead leader," "organizational hierarchy," and "pecking order" make it staunchly clear that one person is on top and that everyone else descends from there. This rhetoric is accepted hook, line, and sinker across the streams of evangelical Christianity.

FUNCTION AND UNCTION

Once again the overwrought concepts of leadership that permeate the contemporary church emphasize leadership from a *positional* viewpoint. This is in stark contrast to the New Testament idea of leadership, which is concerned with *function,* placing the focus on the roles of co-followers rather than their rank. The New Testament places the emphasis on the unction of the Holy Spirit in the lives of men and women who are servants of God and his kingdom initiative rather than on titles and offices. Men and women have dug titles and offices out of the trash heap where Jesus tossed them, shined them up, and hung them on church buildings, office doors, and business cards.

Thinking in terms of verbs rather than nouns is helpful here. John Wimber of the Vineyard movement walked in an apostolic role but refused to be called an apostle. He was extremely concerned to keep the focus of attention on the Holy Spirit and not himself. Wimber wanted to ensure that God received the glory for what may have taken place through him. His emphasis was consistently on the Spirit of God over and above the flesh of humans. For instance, in a training session I once attended, he was asked what elders do, and he said, "Elders eld." Wimber also mentioned that when people asked what they should call him, he would say, "You can call me John. That's what my mother called me." Wimber was not trying to be trite. He just wanted to deemphasize the attention that is so often placed on humans.

Authority as hierarchy always falls short of the glory of God. The reality is that it hijacks God's glory. It is but a mere substitute for relationship, family fellowship, and community. It may be "good business practice," but it is horrific family practice. It was never meant for the household of God, and Jesus emphatically said so. In *The Circle Way*, Christina Baldwin and Ann Linnea write,

> Hierarchy as a model offers an efficient means for charting systems and carrying out specific and repetitive tasks when coordinated effort is required. Hierarchy is useful for passing on information, giving directions, establishing chains of command, developing armies, developing work-forces, organizing data, programming computer software, and mass-producing goods. Yet it lacks a holistic understanding of networked systems and biological interdependence and connectivity.

Within a hierarchical worldview, people look for their place. They can either accept their place as an unchangeable fact or strive ever upward toward greater perceived stability and privilege. That is our heroic story: the rise to power and the escape to greater freedom. The closer people are to the top, the more they tend to accept and defend hierarchy, and the closer people are to the bottom, the more they tend to acquiesce to or resist hierarchy. Every time people enter a meeting we activate the triangle archetype and struggle to find our place within the implied power grid.[6]

OVERSIGHT

Servants who lead help others explore the use of their spiritual gifts, equipping them to be better servants. That is the primary function of leading in the servantship culture of the church. It is much like the role of a parent, an aunt or uncle, or a big brother or sister. It is a joy to help the younger ones learn to walk, to feed themselves, to throw a ball, to plant seeds and pick flowers, or to care for a pet—to learn to live. But leading is not always about the older or more mature ones helping the younger ones. How many of us parents have had to turn to our more tech-savvy children for help in programming an iPod or other electronic device? Leading from a servant posture means learning from anyone, regardless of status or stature. Every member of the body must be allowed to relate to the impulses that come from the Head. The Head (Christ) contains the central nervous system and organizes true order and coordination. To be controlled by a lesser member than the Head is patently dysfunctional.[7]

Of all the joys of parenting for my wife and me, one of our greatest was in observing the differences of our three children and then in helping them develop and use their individual, God-given talents and abilities. From an early age, our son had a tender heart for others, intolerance for injustice, and a desire to help the underdog. At times it was almost impossible to watch a movie as a family because he could not move past certain scenes of injustice or crime against others. He would be asking questions or lamenting out loud about a scene that had happened several minutes earlier. It is no wonder that he has given his life to serving marginalized and downtrodden people in some of the most challenging places in the world.

Our oldest daughter is our artist. She did things with crayons and markers that blew our minds when she was little, and as she entered her teen years, her eye for fashion and ability to create runway ensembles from thrift store clothing was nothing short of amazing. It is no wonder that she has become a hairstylist and makeup artist. The youngest of our children has always amazed us with her industrious will and fortitude. She is the proverbial go-getter. When she sets her mind to accomplish something, you can consider it done. Though she is the youngest of our kids, she acquired her first job before the other two had one. In pursuit of her place in the medical field, she is now attending a university and well on her way to achieving her dream.

For my wife and me, a significant part of our role in parenting our children has been to help them recognize and discover their gifts and talents, training them to steward those abilities for their future. As they became increasingly mature, our oversight adjusted accordingly. We gradually backed off while still keeping an eye on them, reassuring them that we were always available if they needed our help or advice.

OVERSEEING, NOT OVERMANAGING

When authentic relationships do not exist, synthetic replacements and substitutes emerge. In the management ethos of the business sector, making sure employees have clear job descriptions and receive continual inspections of their work performance is common practice. It is not unusual for weekly written reports to be required by managers on the output of workers. This practice has become common in a vast number of churches as well. Weekly written reports are necessary because an ongoing relational dialogue does not exist. There is no way we could imagine our families operating with such a pseudo relational arrangement. Again, such a policy reveals the "we are a business" ideology among churches and leaders that carry on practices such as these.

A lack of genuine relationship necessitates such practices. When there is little to no relational sharing and dialogue the written reports are all you have to work with. But where an overseer has cultivated an ethos of open information flow, the habits are altogether different, such as the case with the pastor that told author George Cladis, "We cram into my office until we're hanging from the rafters, and then we say where we are going, and what we are doing, and what we need from each other, and how we're going to get there, and what we expect from each other. We don't need to write it down."[8]

The New Testament idea of oversight in our churches contains no hint of individuals who have authority over other individuals in the ways we have learned from the systems of the world. In a community governed by oversight rather than by "lording over" others, dialogue and inquiry are welcomed and encouraged, which is a far cry from the message of the Seattle megachurch pastor who preached to his congregation about the issue of "sinning through questioning."

Control is not necessary for order in a living system. What is it that an overseer is to *see* over? It is the life of the person, not merely the work of the person. The life of the staff member should always come before the performance in the order of what the overseer cares about.

This past Christmas was the first in several years in which I was especially excited about what my wife and I were giving our kids. They are all now young adults, and the times of squeals and screams from opening packages of toys are but a distant memory. I was excited because not only were the gifts we bought them what they eagerly wanted but I also wanted them to have the gifts for an especially selfish reason. We had bought them smartphones, and I had each of them install a certain application before leaving the house. It is a tracking application that lets a parent know exactly where a child is at all times.

Our youngest daughter is married, and I don't worry about her as much because she is under the watchful care of her husband. There is also not a tremendous concern about our son, except when he is making a long drive across several states. It is our middle child, our daughter who is single and lives on her own, whom I feel the greatest need to keep an eye on. She works late some nights and has some distance to drive. I don't pester her by calling and texting every time I look at my phone and don't understand why she is where she is. But there have been a few times when I sent a text asking how her day was just to check if she was okay. I did this especially if she was out later than normal. Every week or so if my wife hasn't talked with her, she calls our daughter up just to see how she is doing and if she needs anything.

That is what oversight looks like. It is not dominating or controlling. It is not demanding answers all the time to what, where, and why questions. Our daughter is a responsible and capable adult, with a good head on her shoulders. But for now my wife and I are the main persons in her life who keep an eye on her for the sake of *her*, not for the sake of her performance. We watch *over* her. We don't hover over her or look over her shoulder. We speak into her life and provide counsel and suggestions at times, but there is no commanding and demanding. My wife and I provide oversight in our daughter's life, but she is not *under* our authority. And she appreciates knowing that even though we live almost two hundred miles apart, she is under my watch. It gives her security, and when she needs advice or help with something, she always calls.

MUTUAL ACCOUNTABILITY AND OVERSIGHT

When I was about five years old, I talked my mom into letting me buy a slingshot from the five-and-dime store we stopped at one Saturday afternoon. At first she was reluctant, but my big, brown eyes, a series of long, drawn-out pleases, and a vow to be careful and responsible finally melted her stone-cold resolve. She gave into the purchase. All weekend I shot pebbles at an old tire leaning against a toolshed in our backyard. But by the following Monday I had become bored with shooting at a standing target and was looking for a bigger challenge.

This was the late 1960s, and there were no video games with all the speed and action. But I had an idea. Our house faced a busy thoroughfare that ran through our small town. Looking for a moving target, I found one. Actually, I found a lot of them just by standing in our front yard and shooting at passing cars. It was a great challenge and great fun. That is, until I finally hit one of the speeding cars. As the vehicle skidded to a stop, I dropped my slingshot and headed for cover. I figured the best place to hide would be the bathroom, because no one ever disturbs you when you're in the bathroom, right? There is little point in continuing the story. You can guess what happened next. Authority came down hard on me at the end of a kitchen spatula, and I never saw that slingshot again.

The only way a culture can be led with oversight as opposed to hierarchy is if the individuals on the staffs and teams maintain a commitment to and practice of self-discipline, accountability, and responsibility. Consultant and author Bill Easum emphasizes three characteristics on the part of all involved that are essential for the viability of a trusting servantship environment:

1. *Competency*: Those who function in a team have to be able to count on the other members of the team to do what they say they will do.
2. *Consistency*: They have to be able to count on the other team members to be there for them.
3. *Integrity*: They have to be able to take team members at their word.[9]

Responsibly mature disciples are servants who are faithful and need not be evaluated by a centralized office of command and control. They are constantly submitting themselves to the other members by maintaining a humble posture that invites straightforward critique on an ongoing basis from their peers. Disciples are constantly asking themselves several questions:

- Am I stewarding the resources I have been handed with integrity?
- Is there any pride in me that is keeping me from soliciting advice from others around me?

- Am I being faithful to my call here?
- Is there someone here who could do what I am doing better than I can?

In a servantship community disciples use these same types of questions to lay themselves on the altar of critique before their co-servants. For an oversight culture to work the servant community must consist of self-starters. It takes people who are willing and able to think on their feet, without the need for constant motivation from the outside.

A cautionary tale can be found from World War II. As the tide began to shift and more and more German officers fell in the field of battle, the Allied forces gained an exponential advantage because of the overly hierarchical structure and leadership culture of the Third Reich's military machine. German soldiers who were not officers had never had to make everyday choices, much less moment-by-moment decisions. In fact, they were forbidden to do so. In effect they were little more than cogs in a machine. When the upper ranks were out of the picture, the field soldiers did not know what to do. The American and British soldiers had been trained to think on their own in case of the loss of "official" leaders. They had been equipped to step up and move forward.

HEALTHY CULTURES OF ACCOUNTABILITY

Notice something striking in the following verse, where Paul says he has confidence in the body of Christ to carry out the task of admonishing one another? The letter to the Romans was not addressed to the elders, a senior pastor, or a board or committee. It was written to the priesthood of believers, the community of saints (1:7): "Now I myself am confident concerning you, my brethren, that you also are full of goodness, filled with all knowledge, able also to admonish one another" (15:14, NKJV).

Paul is confident that the goodness, knowledge, and ability to admonish are present in the body itself. He does not say, "You need an executive staff to admonish the lower-level staff members." It is incumbent on the brethren—the siblings (brothers and sisters)—to both warn and exhort one another. The community as a whole has the front-line responsibility for social order and group harmony. Throughout the Epistles, verse after verse underscores the responsibility of the brothers and sisters, the servantship community, to rebuke when necessary and edify at all times. Below are but a sampling of such passages:

- Honor one another—Rom. 12:10
- Build up one another—Rom. 14:19; 1 Thess. 5:11; Heb. 3:13; 10:25
- Warn and exhort one another—Rom. 15:14; Col. 3:16
- Provide discipline among yourselves—1 Cor. 5:3-5
- Bear one another's overwhelming burdens—Gal. 5:13; 6:2
- Submit to one another—Eph. 5:21
- Teach one another—Col. 3:16
- Incite one another to "love and good works"—Heb. 10:24
- Confess sins to one another—James 5:16

Church discipline is not to be carried out by a hierarchical few. It is the responsibility of the everyday saints to carry it out. The responsibility for rebuke, correction, and discipline lies squarely at the feet of the community of saints. Leadership is pastoral care carried out corporately by the entire body. The idea that one person or a select upper echelon of individuals makes all the decisions or handles all the problems lacks biblical support. Frank Viola said it well: "My experience has been that when the fundamental aspects of love and servanthood are mastered in a church, the issues of authority and submission amazingly take care of themselves."[10]

Do you remember that line on your elementary school report card that gauged your ability to cooperate with the other kids—the one with the phrase "plays well with others"? For self-management to hum along, everyone must be willing and eager to value, listen to, and respect the opinions and input of others. People who are stubborn and prideful are not good team players. They are the type of people who have to be managed, if for no other reason than to protect the other kids from their uncooperative ways.

PSEUDO ACCOUNTABILITY

In overly institutionalized, hierarchical cultures, job performance assessment is typically carried out in a most extremely nonrelational fashion, such as the popular 360-degree assessment. Here is how it works: surveys are dispersed to a broad range of people—subordinates, peers, and supervisors—who are promised anonymity in return for their honest answers about the performance of another individual. It has become the regular practice of denominations and churches across America to use such tools. This is another example of worldly practices that fall horrifically short of relational ethos and accountability. Who could conceive of a family bringing a family member into the room and saying, "We can't tell you which family member said you are a selfish, noncontributing, overeating, lazy bum, but that is what has been reported. What do you have to say for yourself?" And then after the "assessment," how could we expect that family member to live with the rest of the family in peace, harmony, trust, and a feeling of safety?

Such thinking is ludicrous. I once watched a friend get assessed this way, and it was one of the cruelest things I have ever witnessed. These types of so-called assessments are void of heart. If someone is not confident enough to look another person in the eye and speak the truth in love, then the relationship is either fragile or the person giving the critique does not possess the intestinal fortitude to be honest. Anonymous assessments have no place in the family of God.

OPENNESS AND HONESTY

Communication is a key component for relationships at any level. If you have ever been married, you are very much aware of the need for good, solid, consistently clear communication. The word "communication" shares its roots with the word "community." Leadership cultures of command and control make it clear to underlings that certain information is to be held close to the vest. Other situations are never to be discussed between staff members—such as disagreements with upper-level leadership decisions.

When information is censored and controlled by a handful of authoritarians at the top of the ladder, a culture of distrust is fostered. It gives our enemy, Satan, the opportunity to do what he does best—sow seeds of division by the use of suspicion and accusation. Many times saints never let accusations cross their lips, but they still make lengthy speeches in their minds.

One former staff member of a church that was led by the hierarchy of a senior pastor and executive pastor shared an interesting story. He had received a harsh phone call from the senior pastor after he had sent an email to the executive pastor taking issue with the Christmas weekend church schedule. The schedule had been announced without any input from staff members. It meant they would all be working on both Christmas Eve and Christmas Day. He was offering an alternative solution and had an idea about how to make it happen. The senior pastor called him and asked him if he had been "polling" other staff members and warned him that if he had, it would be grounds for serious discipline.

Censoring and controlling information and knowledge are essential for maintaining a dominant culture. But they have no place in a servantship culture. They have no place in the household of Christ. True community is impossible without a significantly trusting culture expressed through attitudes, habits, and beliefs. Where trust exists, there is little need for a myriad of checks and balances that create staff policies and procedures. The main rule should be, "Permission granted!"

When a trusting community culture exists, creativity and responsibility course through the life of the body. Failure *is* an option. There is collective ownership of the vision by the community of saints. The accomplishment of the vision is not regulated, dominated, or commandeered by one or a few higher-ups. Teams begin to form, and life explodes through the collective gifts and talents of the men and women God has called together. They become the "living stones" spoken of by the apostle Peter: "You yourselves like living stones are being built up as a spiritual house, to be a holy priesthood, to offer spiritual sacrifices acceptable to God through Jesus Christ" (1 Pet. 2:5).

My friend Kim Hammond serves on the team at Community Christian Church in Naperville, Illinois. Shortly after he began serving there, he told me about the leadership culture at Community Christian and how inclusive and flattened it was. Over a couple of years Kim kept telling me, "You've got to visit one of the monthly leadership community meetings. They throw chairs and stuff. It's crazy." I asked him what he meant by throwing chairs. Kim said emphatically, "Dude, I'm telling you. They throw chairs." Recently I happened to be visiting Kim on a day Community Christian was having its leadership community gathering, and I was invited to sit in. Understand that this is a multisite church and that the leaders from almost all the surrounding church staffs gather together. There were probably close to a hundred people gathered in a quaint theatre-style room.

The meeting had the feel of a pep rally, and at first I thought it might be a bit cheesy, like an Amway rally. That was not the case at all. There was a tangible spirit of authentic camaraderie that permeated the place. It was obviously an event these folks looked forward to and relished. Raucous applause greeted the reports they gave of their labors—and yes, they threw chairs. An announcement would be made, reporting an accomplishment or a new team member who had come on board, and chairs would start flying down the aisles as hoots and shouts filled the room. No big personality dominated the meeting. No big vision-casting talk issued from Dave and John (the founding pastors). Stories were told and prayers were prayed. It was a true community family affair.

FIVE TYPES OF AUTHORITY

In his excellent book *Organic Leadership,* Neil Cole mentions five types of authority that we most often encounter:

1. *Positional authority* is derived from the rank or place one occupies in a system or organization. It is tied directly to the chain of command. With positional authority, the amount of respect a person has is based on the position alone. Many times those who show respect to a person in positional authority do not actually respect the person as much as they fear the position.

2. *Expertise authority* comes via the experience, knowledge, or learned skill a person has in a certain field. This person may not hold a particular title or position. He or she is respected in his or her field of expertise only. It is a very limited form of authority.

3. *Relational authority* is based on who a person is as that person relates to others around him or her. The greater degree of love and respect others have for this person is the degree of authority he or she has. Those who know this person respect him or her and open the door of their lives based on personal respect.

4. *Moral authority* is possessed by one who others respect on the basis of his or her reputation as a person of integrity, with moral fiber and truthfulness. As long as people believe they can trust this person, the moral authority remains. If trust is shaken or the reputation disintegrates, the authority goes with it. Moral authority can take a lifetime to gain and be lost in a day or less.

5. *Spiritual authority* is the strongest type of authority. No one can earn spiritual authority, because it comes from God and only he can grant it. God uses people with this type of authority by speaking through them. Their authority is not autonomous but comes as God wills in the moment.[11]

Positional authority is the weakest type of authority. Neil Cole writes, "This authority has little to do with who you are but is more about your place in the organization. Granted, position is not given to just anyone; it usually has to be earned. But all of us have dealt with someone who would not be given respect if it were not for his or her position."[12]

THE ATTITUDE OF AND TOWARD AUTHORITY

For most of us, growing up, we quickly learned what the word "obey" meant. It meant "Do what you're told." At times it meant "Do it and do it now, or face the consequences." I can't count the times I have heard the following verse quoted as a proof text for hierarchical leadership: "Obey your leaders and submit to them, for they are keeping watch over your souls, as those who will have to give an account. Let them do this with joy and not with groaning, for that would be of no advantage to you" (Heb. 13:17).

The message seems clear enough: "Do what your leaders tell you to do." But that is not the message we hear when we look at the definition of the Greek word translated "obey" in this verse. It is not the often used *hypakouō*, which means "to hearken to a command." And it is not *peitharcheō*, which means "to obey a superior." The word translated "obey" in this verse is *peithō*, which means "to be persuaded by." The author of Hebrews is pleading for the saints to be persuaded by those who are of deeper spiritual maturity.

This verse is addressing the attitude of the one being overseen by the other person. The writer is calling for a humble posture. If the person in authority is using his or her authority from a posture of humility as well, great things take place. Jesus always went for the heart. He was most concerned with motives, because motives determine direction. Again, there certainly are those in the body who have authority. Throughout his letters, Paul goes to great lengths, as does Jesus, to make clear how authority is to be handled in the body of Christ. The very persona of how to handle the responsibility of authority and oversight is captured wonderfully by Paul in his letter to the Philippians. We have quoted these verses earlier, but they bear repeating here:

> Do nothing out of rivalry or conceit, but in humility consider others as more important than yourselves. Everyone should look out not only for his own interests, but also for the interests of others. Make your own attitude that of Christ Jesus, who, existing in the form of God, did not consider equality with God as something to be used for His own advantage. Instead He emptied Himself by assuming the form of a slave, taking on the likeness of men. And when He had come as a man in His external form, He humbled Himself by becoming obedient to the point of death—even to death on a cross. (Phil. 2:3-8, HCSB)

We can find no better example of servantship than Jesus himself. Volumes have been written on this passage, but our present concern has to do with the issue of the use of power. Notice the phrase "something to be used for His own advantage" (v. 6, HCSB). The NRSV translation renders it as "something to be exploited." Paul is emphasizing that though Jesus possessed the very power of God, he refused to exploit it. He refused to wield that power. Jesus did not regard his power as an opportunity to use it to his advantage. The reason Paul wrote this passage in the first place lies in the preceding phrase, "Make your own attitude that of Christ Jesus" (v. 5, HCSB). He is telling us all to maintain the attitude of Jesus. You may be a leader with the positional power or authority to operate in ways that are advantageous to you. Paul says if you do so, you are not following Jesus.

The chart below is a list of descriptor words that provide hints or clues as to the type of culture—hierarchy or oversight—that exists in an organization, church, or ministry.

Hierarchy	Oversight
Jesus called them to him and said, "You know that the rulers of the Gentiles lord it over them, and their great ones exercise authority over them. It shall not be so among you." (Matt. 20:25-26*a*)	"But whoever would be great among you must be your servant, and whoever would be first among you must be your slave, even as the Son of Man came not to be served but to serve, and to give his life as a ransom for many." (Matt. 20:26*b*-28)
Suspicion	Confidence
Caution	Risk
Either/Or	Both/And
Mine	Ours
Certainty	Mystery
Position	Relationship
Dictate	Collaborate
Win	Win/Win
Manage	Guide
Hold	Release
Fear	Trust
Intellect	Holy Spirit
Boss	Mentor
Staff	Peers
Pyramid	Circle
Hoard	Share
Inspect	Review
Rank	Role

Demand	Suggest
Command	Request
Rules	Guidelines
Subjugate	Elevate
Criticize	Counsel
Monologue	Dialogue
Regulation	Reasoning
Intimidate	Encourage
Assignments	Agreements
Conformity	Diversity
Departments	Holistic
Control	Permission
Censor	Broadcaster
Supervision	Self-control

SEVEN

FOLLOW THE UNLEADER
REIMAGINING DISCIPLE MAKING

How did I get to the place where I was so off-task, caring more about my church's "organizational extension and survival" and measuring success in business terms—attendance, buildings and cash—rather than in becoming and making mature disciples of Jesus? How did church become more of a business organization for consumers of religious goods and services than a training ground of followers of Jesus?

—Keith Meyer[1]

To follow means to follow, not to lead. To point not to our own superior moral character but to the dimly seen figure out there that we are stumbling after.

—Frederick Buechner[2]

Who discipled you?" This is a question I have asked a lot of Christians. It's fascinating but terribly sad that many or most Christians and leaders cannot name someone who personally discipled them. At age nineteen, having grown up as a Christian but having walked away from any interest in the things of the Lord, I had an amazing prodigal-like encounter. For years I had frequented my parent's small down-home church, and at the time of my return to the Lord, this little congregation was experiencing quite a revival. Over a period of two years it had begun to grow, and there was a real excitement about what the Holy Spirit might do each Sunday morning. Every week the church was packed to the walls. The pastor had a strong preaching gift, delivering inspiring themes that were taking root in the hearts of the people, and there was a feeling of electricity in the air almost all the time.

I joined a small-group Bible study, totally immersed myself in the Bible, and began listening to cassette tapes (remember those?) of sermons. I read everything I could get my hands on, trying my best to develop myself as a follower of Jesus. Intuitively though, I knew I needed help. I needed someone to guide me, someone to help me process my walk, but no one offered to help.

It seemed to me the best person to help me was the pastor. His preaching was inspiring, he appeared to know and understand the Bible better than anyone else around, and he was friendly and down to earth. I'll never forget the first time I approached him about getting together to begin a one-on-one process of guiding me. I didn't know what to call what I was asking for. I just needed someone more experienced to help me. I explained that I was doing everything I knew to do but still felt I needed someone to guide me along. For the first time I had ever seen it happen, the pastor was fumbling for words. The color left his face for a moment, replaced with a reddish flush, and he appeared to have an instant case of dry mouth, swallowing hard between the few words he squeezed out. To his credit he agreed to meet with me weekly, but after three awkward meetings he told me he thought I was good to go on my own. "Just keep reading the Word, and the Holy Spirit will guide you along," he said. I can still remember the relief on his face as I left his house that last time.

Here was a guy I had heard sermonize countless times for over an hour at a time, with confidence, poise, and clear and concise points. But each time we got together one-on-one, he seemed dazed and confused, struggling for direction and conversation. He was totally uncomfortable. As a young person who had just made a commitment to following Jesus, this was a tremendously confusing and disappointing experience. Looking back on it now, I realize this pastor was simply freaked out by the prospect of discipling someone. He clearly didn't know how to do it, and I do not lay the blame at his feet, because most likely no one had ever done it for him. This gifted preacher had probably never been discipled, and he had no clue about how to disciple someone else.

THE GREATEST FOLLOWER

Jesus was a follower. That may sound like borderline blasphemy to some. It may be hard for you to think of Jesus as a follower. Especially in a culture such as ours, which looks down on the idea of being a follower, it's difficult for us to think of Jesus as one. The truth is that not only was he a follower but he was the greatest follower in all of history.

When we think of great leaders, our minds drift to the great innovators—groundbreaking inventors and paradigm-shifting philosophers throughout the ages—Socrates, Plato, Edison, Einstein, Henry Ford, and so on. More recently, we look to technology icons such as Bill Gates and Steve Jobs. Shockingly, Jesus identified himself not as a leader but as a follower. In fact, he said he had no original ideas:

I can do nothing on my own. As I hear, I judge, and my judgment is just, because I seek not my own will but the will of him who sent me. . . .

. . . For I have not spoken on my own authority, but the Father who sent me has himself given me a commandment—what to say and what to speak. And I know that his commandment is eternal life. What I say, therefore, I say as the Father has told me. (John 5:30; 12:49-50)

Jesus followed the Father. He walked in the steps and direction the Lord told him to go. He judged according to the will of God. He spoke the words the Father told him to speak, and his authority came from following God. But Jesus did have a "strategic" plan. We see it in Mark 3:14: "And he appointed twelve (whom he also named apostles) so that they might *be with him*" (emphasis added).

Jesus' idea of making disciples was to invite a group of people to join him in life. He didn't invite them to a Bible study, a small-group meeting, or even to a men's accountability group—all of which can contribute to disciple making. But those activities will never get the job of disciple making done without the vital component of a more seasoned, mature disciple. Such a person is needed to invite others to come along with him or her so they can experience the way a disciple actually lives his or her life. There is no substitute for this. To develop disciples nothing can replace the effectiveness of coming alongside and *being with* the more experienced follower of Jesus. And this can only take place among a small number of people.

Eating together, playing together, praying together—this is what it means to "be with" someone. The leadership-centric culture in most churches has people at the top of the ladder who cannot point to a group of people they have invited to "be with" them in life for the purpose of discipleship.

The distance between upper-echelon church leaders and others betrays the reality that there is no authentic discipling relationship in play. Nannerl Keohane, former president of Duke University, writes,

When we speak of "relationships," we usually have in mind close, affectionate, enduring affiliations with a parent, lover, husband, sibling, colleague, or friend. The distinctive connection between leaders and followers is not well captured by this term. In large organizations leaders have many followers; followers have only one leader (or a small number of leaders). The followers may feel that they "know" the leader through observing her in action, shaking her hand at a large gathering, receiving a certificate of commendation, or reading about the leader's family. On this basis, if they generally approve the leader's actions and sense any kind of personal warmth on the leader's part, they are indeed likely to feel that they do indeed have a direct, personal connection with the leader. But no leader can have a direct, personal connection with large numbers of followers; this is possible only for those with whom [she] works most immediately. Occasional personal encounters with other followers can be meaningful to the leader, but they are rarely as important as they are for the follower. These "relationships" cannot, by their very nature, be symmetrical. So the connection between the leader and her followers must be more abstract, detached, and impersonal than the term "relationship" can usefully be expected to describe.[3]

OUR CURRENT SITUATION

Every statistical study over the past forty years clearly shows that Western culture is in the midst of a complete moral collapse. Though we have more and bigger churches, more and bigger conferences, more teaching, more books—Christianity is not transforming Western culture. Dallas Willard says,

Nondiscipleship is the elephant in the church. It is not the much discussed moral failures, financial abuses, or the amazing general similarity between Christians and non-Christians. These are only effects of the underlying problem. The fundamental negative reality among Christian believers now is their failure to be constantly learning how to live their lives in The Kingdom Among Us.[4]

In agreement with Willard, we are convinced that the lost art of disciple making must be rediscovered and replanted into the heart and psyche of the church if we are to have any hope of making a kingdom impact in the West. Alan and Debra Hirsch emphasize the followership crisis before us:

> Our lives, individual and corporate, play a vital role in the unfolding of the grand purposes of God. More is at stake in discipleship than our own personal salvation. The gospel cannot be limited to being about my personal healing and wholeness, but rather extends in and through my salvation to the salvation of the world. To fail in discipleship and disciple-making is therefore to fail in the primary mission (or "sentness") of the church. And it does not take a genius to realize that we have all but lost the art of disciple-making in the contemporary Western church.[5]

PREACHING IS NOT THE ANSWER

We have massive bookstores and libraries of information on what a disciple is. But if you search for information on how to *make* a disciple, well, that's another matter. We have reduced the Great Commission to a treatise on salvation. How puzzling that is in the light of Jesus' command to give ourselves wholly to training disciples: "And Jesus came and said to them, 'All authority in heaven and on earth has been given to me. Go therefore and make disciples of all nations, baptizing them in the name of the Father and of the Son and of the Holy Spirit, teaching them to observe all that I have commanded you. And behold, I am with you always, to the end of the age'" (Matt. 28:18-20).

Jesus' words are commissioning his followers not merely to make converts to or to give lectures on a belief system but to do with others what he had done with them, following his pattern and model. There is no substitute for this. When we unpack Jesus' disciple-making modus operandi, we see Jesus giving three years of his life, sharing his personal journey with God with a group of others. Reading through the Gospels we see Jesus doing a lot of eating with his disciples, a lot of praying, and a lot of healing others—a lot of serving. After he taught the crowds, he would get alone with his disciples and unpack the "sermon," asking them what they heard, how they perceived what he had said. He taught servantship through followership. The result was a group of people that became disciples and turned their world upside down.

Jesus invited his followers to get the dirt of ministry under their fingernails by pushing them into situations where they had to take the reins and do the serving, casting out of demons and laying hands on the sick. And he would do follow-up by debriefing them after their experiences. No, this was not *teaching* and *preaching*; it was *training*. It included teaching, but it went way beyond that.

The issue of disciple making and what it means to be and to make authentic followers of Jesus is probably the most vital factor in the shaping of our church's culture and mission. We have proven our ability to amass large groups of people in church buildings, but to fail in servant/disciple making through followership is the ultimate failure of all. C. S. Lewis was on target when he said that the paramount purpose of the church was to create little Christs. He said, "If the Church is not doing this, then all the cathedrals, clergy, missions, sermons, even the Bible, are a waste of time."[6] Jesus invited his followers into a process that was more apprentice-like than classroom-like. He formed a life-as-laboratory culture in which ideas and theories were practiced and tested rather than merely preached and taught. His was a community of disciples, where the newly converted followed the previously converted in a new way of doing life.

STUDY GROUPS ARE NOT THE ANSWER

Imagine this scenario. You are a parent of a recently born baby girl, and unfortunately the doctors discover the infant has a small hole in her heart, but they assure you surgery can correct the issue and recommend a particular surgeon. Straight-away you schedule an appointment with the surgeon and show up to meet her. At this meeting you engage in a conversation that revolves around the doctor's experience and background. She shares that she has never actually practiced in a hospital or doctor's office before opening her own practice. Gleefully though, she shows you a wall of books she has faithfully studied and shares that every Thursday night she is in a "heart surgeon's handbook" study group. Needless to say, there would be no way you would let this surgeon anywhere near your child. The same type of scenario could be set to the idea of a car mechanic, an electrician or a plumber working on your house, or a carpenter hired to add a room to your house.

We expect doctors and trade professionals to have spent a sufficient amount of time as apprentices to more experienced doctors and master craftspeople. It is not enough to have read books or heard lectures on a subject. Studying is but one aspect of learning. Hands-on training is absolutely essential to develop core competencies in any subject or skill. It is past time we realize we have been given the responsibility of bringing believers into maturity, and we cannot continue to serve up more Bible study as an answer for making disciples.

We must resist a posture that says, "Let the Scriptures make disciples." The Bible is the Word of God—a *follow me* Word that must be demonstrated if disciples are to emerge from exposure to it. Bible studies are an essential part of the ongoing discipleship process, but "part" is the operative word here. They are only one tool within the disciple-making process. Many church leaders will point to the menu of Bible studies their church has when asked to describe their disciple-making process. This is tantamount to a restaurant that only serves recipes. The Bible teaches us how to make a life cultivated in God.

FOLLOW ME

We need real, breathing, walking-around, hands-and-feet, human examples—followers who are following Jesus. This is essential and without substitute. The example of Jesus, alive in the framework of living flesh and blood, gives the greatest reference for potential followers to follow. Jesus demonstrates that the gospel message is something that can tangibly be lived. Teaching and preaching will never bring this about. We need proof to show us not only that it *can* still be lived out but also *how* to live it out.

Young converts need to hang out with seasoned disciples in relationships that cause them to frequently say to themselves, "Oh, that's what following Jesus looks like." The very idea that one believer would say to another, "Follow me" or "Imitate me," is not only lost in most forms of contemporary Christianity but also might even be considered arrogant, cultish, and downright scandalous to many. Yet this type of mentoring relationship is the very essence of discipleship. Paul Stanley and Bobby Clinton convey this idea:

> Mentoring is as old as civilization itself. Through this natural relational process, experience and values pass from one generation to another. Mentoring took place among Old Testament prophets (Eli and Samuel, Elijah and Elisha) and leaders (Moses and Joshua), and New Testament leaders (Barnabas and Paul, Paul and Timothy). Throughout human history, mentoring was the primary means of passing on knowledge and skills in every field—from Greek philosophers to sailors—and in every culture. But in the modern age, the learning shifted. It now relies primarily on computers, classrooms, books, and videos. Thus, today the relational connection between the knowledge-and-experience giver and the receiver has weakened or is nonexistent.[7]

The pattern and ethos of Jesus-style discipleship revolves around the idea that it is disciples who in turn make disciples. According to the New Testament pattern, pastors, church programs, and preaching alone are not what make disciples. No, it is very clear that Jesus intended that *all* of his followers become disciples and then in turn be disciple makers, regardless of their vocation.

The "follow me" framework of disciple making is one of the most integral cogs for carrying out the Great Commission. We must cease kidding ourselves that anything less than the "imitate me" mode will result in more than what we are currently achieving—an unchanged church and an unchanged world. The early church brand of discipleship demanded followers who were follow-worthy. The early catechisms were clear on this matter; anything short of this standard meant being denied entry into the Jesus community.

THE UNLEADER INITIATIVE

The most prolific of the New Testament writers, Paul, includes riffs of the imitate-follow-copy theme throughout his letters, as the following passages from the *New American Standard Bible* demonstrate (italics added):

Therefore I exhort you, *be imitators of me.* For this reason I have sent to you Timothy, who is my beloved and faithful child in the Lord, and he will remind you of my ways which are in Christ, just as I teach everywhere in every church. (1 Cor. 4:16-17)

Be imitators of me, just as I also am of Christ. (1 Cor. 11:1)

Brethren, join in *following my example,* and observe those who walk according to the pattern you have in us. (Phil. 3:17)

The things you have *learned and received and heard and seen in me,* practice these things, and the God of peace will be with you. (Phil. 4:9)

You also *became imitators* of us and of the Lord, having received the word in much tribulation with the joy of the Holy Spirit. (1 Thess. 1:6)

Nor did we eat anyone's bread without paying for it, but with labor and hardship we kept working night and day so that we would not be a burden to any of you; not because we do not have the right to this, but in order to offer ourselves as a model for you, so that you would *follow our example.* (2 Thess. 3:8-9)

The things which you have heard from me in the presence of many witnesses, entrust these to faithful men who will be able to teach others also. (2 Tim. 2:2)

Paul's invitation was to follow him on his journey of following Christ. He was not implying that he was a perfect man. His letters made it clear that Christ, and Christ alone, was the only Source of righteousness. What he *was* saying is that Jesus, living in a follower, is an observable, tangible fact, and that new believers become disciples by associating and relating closely with followers on the path ahead of them. The letters to the early church reveal that the means of developing followers of Christ were not situated primarily in the activities of preaching and Bible studies.

The Epistles portray a people who added discipline to the flow of their lives, along with their learning and Scripture study. We see discipleship as a learning process that joined nascent believers to more experienced believers. These more mature followers were not merely *telling* others how to live the life but also *showing* them how to live it. All of us—pastors, church planters, leaders in churches, and church members—need to ask some hard questions: "Does my church set this as its main goal?" "Are we challenging one another to do this?" "Does our church provide the opportunity for newer believers to be apprenticed by more experienced believers?"

Earlier I shared my experience as a young believer in search of someone to disciple me. Fortunately, shortly after my misadventure with the pastor who was shell-shocked by the idea of mentoring someone, the Lord brought another man into my life to guide me. Sam Spence was the son of a legendary Texas cutting-horse trainer. He and his wife, Margie, had become Christians several years before I met them, and they planted and pastored a small but vibrant country church on the outskirts of Fort Worth. Although I was less than half his age, Sam befriended me and took me under his wing. He never said, "Follow me"; he just began to invite me along as he followed Jesus. Sam would call me up and say, "Hey, partner, I'm taking some groceries over to the Smiths, an elderly couple who are having a tough time. Wanna come along?" Or "You want to go with me to pray with this guy? He's had a real battle with the bottle, and his wife has just let him know she's had enough and is leaving him."

I did some really knuckleheaded stuff, and there is no doubt in my mind that on many occasions Sam must have thought his dad never had to tame and train a wilder mustang than me. I embarrassed and frustrated him many times I *was* aware of, and I can only fathom how many times I did the same but remained clueless to it. But like a patient horse whisperer, he never jerked the reins or cracked a whip. What Sam did with me was not programmed or dictated. He simply invited me into his life; he included me in the natural ebb and flow of not only church stuff and ministry but also life itself—his life. I'm not even sure he knew he was discipling me at the time.

I was able to watch Sam and Margie up close as they raised a household of kids, constantly gave possessions, finances, and resources of all kind to others, and shared the gospel and their faith day by day. I would be hard pressed to name all the people in need whom they let live at their home for extended periods of time. Sam not only gave me opportunities to preach and teach but more importantly was a living example of what it looked like to live out the fruit of the Spirit—gentleness, meekness, patience, mercy, kindness, joy, peace, and so on. He taught me what it meant to lead with a gentle wisdom that was not over-bearing, demanding, and dictatorial but caused you to want to follow Jesus. Sam's leadership-discipling style was a mixture of father, big brother, and friend—all rolled up into one.

I spent about four years with Sam, and it's been over two decades since we worked together side by side. Years at a time have gone by without a chance for us to talk or see one another because of geographical distance and the busyness of life. But to this very day there are times I find myself in situations where

I stop to think, "How would Sam handle this?" or "How would Sam respond to what that person just said?"

It was not that he had become a can-do-no-wrong hero for me, but Sam was a flesh-and-blood person who embodied and modeled the character of Jesus for me in living color, over an extended period of time and through many real-life crises. I'm not sure I could give you the title or even a handful of points to any of the hundreds of sermons I heard Sam preach, but I could certainly go on for hours sharing what he taught me while I was *with him*. In reflecting over my own life as a church planter and pastor, the greatest joy I have experienced and the best fruit has been in my relationships with men and women, young and old, whom I've invited into my life to *be with me*, just as Sam had invited me to be with him.

This is what it looks like to disciple someone. And you don't have to be a pastor or "official" leader in a church to do this. One of the major blockages to widespread followership comes from the belief by most Christians that they are not *expected* to be discipling others. The belief is that *leaders* are the disciplers. Satan could not have crafted a more deceitful scheme than this bogus idea. By convincing the majority of Christians that they have no significant part to play in disciple making, he short-circuits the movement ethos of Christianity. This may be a new concept to some who read this, but truthfully if you are a Christian, you are called and commissioned by Jesus Christ to make disciples.

Unleaders are willing to bare their souls. They are people who are not afraid to be known outside the walls of the church building. Hear the words of the apostle:

> Even though we had some standing as Christ's apostles, we never threw our weight around or tried to come across as important, with you or anyone else. We weren't aloof with you. We took you just as you were. We were never patronizing, never condescending, but we cared for you the way a mother cares for her children. We loved you dearly. Not

content to just pass on the Message, we wanted to give you our hearts. And we did. (1 Thess. 2:6-8, TM)

In the Jesus culture of servantship, the most important metrics and "deliverables" we can observe lie in the transformed lives of the disciples we are making—servants who serve one another and serve the world, doing it all for the glory of God. The real fruit of our churches lies not in the number of people we have the ability to amass one day a week. It lies in what is happening in the lives of those who have gathered. The greatest joy of a church servant should be to see new Christ followers demonstrating love for each other. The apostle Paul spoke of his bragging to other churches about what he was seeing among the believers in Thessalonica: "We ought always to give thanks to God for you, brothers, as is right, because your faith is growing abundantly, and the love of every one of you for one another is increasing. Therefore we ourselves boast about you" (2 Thess. 1:3-4a).

Unleaders are followers of Jesus who invite others to follow them into a life of servantship. Unleaders shun titles and applause and find their greatest joy in shining the light on the supreme beauty and wonder of Jesus Christ. Unleaders refuse to touch, much less hijack, his glory. They serve God in humility and obscurity as much as possible. Unleaders treat their fellow servants with mutual honor and respect, as peers and co-followers of Christ. They embrace the family of God as a covenant of kindred fellowship. Unleaders follow Jesus, embracing the towel and basin of serving along the journey.

UNLEADER—A BENEDICTION

It has been noted in various quarters that the half-illiterate Italian violin maker Antonio Stradivari never recorded the exact plans or dimensions for how to make one of his famous instruments. This might have been a commercial decision (during the earliest years of the 1700s, Stradivari's violins were in high demand and open to being copied by other luthiers). But it might also have been because, well, Stradivari didn't *know* exactly how to record its dimensions, its weight, and its balance. I mean, he knew how to create a violin with his hands and his fingers but maybe not in figures he kept in his head.

Today, those violins, named after the Latinized form of his name, Stradivarius, are considered priceless. It is believed there are only around five hundred of them still in existence, some of which have been submitted to the most intense scientific examination in an attempt to reproduce their extraordinary sound quality. But no one has been able to replicate Stradivari's craftsmanship.

They've worked out that he used spruce for the top, willow for the internal blocks and linings, and maple for the back, ribs, and neck. They've figured out that he also treated the wood with several types of minerals, including potassium borate, sodium and potassium silicate, as well as a handmade varnish that appears to have been composed of gum arabic, honey, and egg white. But they still can't replicate a Stradivarius.

The genius craftsman never once recorded his technique for posterity. Instead, he passed on his knowledge to a number of his apprentices through what the philosopher Michael Polyani called "elbow learning." This is the process where a protégé is trained in a new art or skill by sitting at the elbow of a master and by learning the craft through *doing* it, *copying* it, not simply by reading about it.

The apprentices of the great Stradivari didn't learn their craft from books or manuals but by sitting at his elbow and feeling the wood as he felt it to assess its length, its balance, and its timbre right there in their fingertips. All the learning happened at his elbow, and all the knowledge was contained in his fingers.

In his book *Personal Knowledge*, Polyani wrote, "Practical wisdom is more truly embodied in action than expressed in rules of action."[1] By that he meant that we learn as Stradivari's protégés did, by feeling the weight of a piece of wood, not by reading the prescribed measurements in a manual. Polyani continues,

> To learn by example is to submit to authority. You follow your master because you trust his manner of doing things even when you cannot analyze and account in detail for its effectiveness. By watching the master and emulating his efforts in the presence of his example, the apprentice unconsciously picks up the rules of the art, including those which are not explicitly known to the master himself. These hidden rules can be assimilated only by a person who surrenders himself to that extent uncritically to the imitation of another.[2]

This is the way of the unleader as Lance Ford has described it. Instead of churning out books, manuals, DVDs, podcasts, websites, tweets, and status updates, the unleader takes a band of protégés to his or her elbow and humbly, but relentlessly, passes on the "hidden rules" of service. True leaders model it, live it, breathe it, and invite others to copy them. In this vein, Lance quotes Paul writing to the Corinthians, "Be imitators of me, as I am of Christ" (1 Cor. 11:1). Now that's elbow learning.

This is how we should learn to serve the Master. Indeed, this is how the Master himself "apprenticed" his disciples. Far from teaching them the "measurements" of ministry, he sat them at his elbow and invited them to submit uncritically to his authority. That's how churches should grow leaders—by taking emerging leaders to their elbows and modeling the "hidden rules" of ministry.

As Lance Ford says in chapter 7,

We need real, breathing, walking-around, hands-and-feet, human examples—followers who are following Jesus. This is essential and without substitute. The example of Jesus, alive in the framework of living flesh and blood, gives the greatest reference for potential followers to follow. Jesus demonstrates that the gospel message is something that can tangibly be lived.

Compare this to the apocryphal story of the young Albert Einstein travelling through Europe on a lecture tour of the great universities. He had employed one of his doctoral students to accompany him as his general assistant and driver. At each school, Einstein delivered exactly the same lecture on the application of his general theory of relativity to model the structure of the universe as a whole. This became increasingly monotonous for both the professor and his student driver, and so to alleviate the boredom Einstein and his protégé decided to mix things up a bit at the next lecture by switching places. Einstein was not yet internationally famous, so no one would know if his student appeared on the platform instead of him. The student had heard the presentation scores of times, so he could deliver it as faultlessly as his teacher.

At the next university the student passed himself off to their hosts as Einstein, and the great scientist was introduced as his student and driver. No one was any the wiser. Indeed, no one knew anything was amiss during the lecture, which the student delivered flawlessly while Einstein sat smirking in the front row. However, at the end of the presentation, the host professor did something that no other host had done during the lecture tour. He invited the audience to ask questions.

The blood drained from the fake Einstein's face as a physics professor in the audience asked a particularly difficult question having to do with problems of statistical mechanics and quantum theory, particle theory, and the motion of molecules. Einstein himself blanched, knowing the game was up. Then the student composed himself and continued the ruse: "That question is so simple it insults my intelligence. And to prove it I'm going to ask my chauffeur to answer it."[3]

Stradivari's protégés knew how to make a violin because they had sat at their master's elbow, they had imbibed all that he knew about his craft, and they had measured every aspect of the instrument with their own hands after watching him measure it with his. Einstein's student knew how to recite a lecture without knowing all there was to know about the theory of relativity.

I fear we are living through a time in the church's history when once again leadership has been reduced to simple steps or memorable formulas, when authors are purveying models they claim anyone can quickly adopt, and when conference speakers are dishing up five of their seven steps for effective leadership and then encouraging audiences to buy their latest book for the last two steps. But too many so-called leaders only know one lecture's worth of material. They need their fingertips to be dried out by the handling of spruce and for their nostrils to be filled with willow sawdust. They need to sit for hours on end at their Master's workbench to humble themselves enough to learn, to suffer, to sacrifice, to be shaped into the likeness of the Master Craftsman.

I agree with Lance Ford when he calls us to embrace un-leadership and the downward path that leads to the elbow of the Master. The book you are holding right now is an invitation to adopt a radical new stance on Christian leadership. As Alan Hirsch says in his foreword, "If *UnLeader* does contain a prophetic challenge, and I . . . believe it does, then, like all prophetic texts, we ignore it to our peril." I couldn't agree more.

—*Michael Frost*
Vice Principal (Faculty Development)
Morling College, Sydney

NOTES

PART I—INTRODUCTION

1. "Memorable Quotes for *The Matrix*," IMDb.com, http://www
.imdb.com/title/tt0133093/quotes?qt=qt0324256 (accessed April 16,
2012).

CHAPTER 1

1. Scott A. Bessenecker, *How to Inherit the Earth: Submitting
Ourselves to a Servant Savior* (Downers Grove, IL: InterVarsity Press,
2009), 53.

2. Rusty Ricketson, *Follower First: Rethinking Leading in the
Church* (Cumming, GA: Heartworks Publications, 2009), 48.

3. Brant Hansen, "More Excepts from the 417 Rules of Awesomely
Bold Leadership: 'Lead, Follow . . . or Get out of My Seminar,'" *Letters
from Camp Krusty* (blog), January 2009, http://branthansen.typepad
.com/letters_from_kamp_krusty/page/7/ (accessed May 1, 2012). Used
by permission.

4. Brant Hansen, "More Excerpts from the 417 Rules of Awesomely
Bold Leadership: Lead Through Endless Talking About Leading," *Letters from Camp Krusty* (blog), May 2008, http://branthansen.typepad
.com/letters_from_kamp_krusty/2008/05/more-excerpts-f.html (accessed May 1, 2012). Used by permission.

5. Barbara Kellerman, *Followership: How Followers Are Creating
Change and Changing Leaders* (Boston: Harvard Business School Press,
2008), xvii.

6. Ibid., 6.

7. Robert Earl Kelley, *The Power of Followership: How to Create
Leaders People Want to Follow, and Followers Who Lead Themselves*
(New York: Doubleday/Currency, 1992), 34.

8. Neil Cole, *Organic Leadership: Leading Naturally Right Where
You Are* (Grand Rapids: Baker Books, 2009), 61.

9. Ed Stetzer, "7 Issues Church Planters Face, Issue #1—Leadership Development and Reproducing Culture," *The Lifeway Research
Blog*, January 12, 2011, http://www.edstetzer.com/2011/01/7-top-issues
-church-planters-f.html (accessed May 1, 2012).

10. Ed Stetzer, "7 Issues Church Planters Face, Issue #4—System, Processes and Cultures," *The Lifeway Research Blog*, January 26, 2011, http://www.edstetzer.com/2011/01/7-top-issues-planters-face-iss.html (accessed May 1, 2012).

11. Todd Wilson, "What If," *Future Travelers*, Exponential, January 25, 2011, http://www.exponential.org/2011/01/what-if/ (site discontinued; see reposting at *Brian's Blog*, April 23, 2011, http://web.me.com/ brian_carol/The_Rochester_Connection_Official_Site/Brians _Ministry_Blog/Entries/2011/4/23_What_if%E2%80%A6.html [accessed May 11, 2012]).

12. "Memorable Quotes for *The Shawshank Redemption*," IMDb .com, http://www.imdb.com/title/tt0111161/quotes (accessed April 17, 2012).

CHAPTER 2

1. Mike Breen, "Why Corporate Church Won't Work," Verge Network, http://www.vergenetwork.org/2012/01/02/why-corporate-church -wont-work-mike-breen/ (accessed April 18, 2012).

2. Cole, *Organic Leadership*, 96.

3. Editor's note: This interpretation of the Nicolaitans is just one possibility. There are several other interpretations that have received strong support from biblical scholars. Many commentators have concluded that the Nicolaitans practiced immorality and held Gnostic beliefs; also, church tradition teaches that there is a connection between this group and the deacon Nicolas mentioned in Acts 6:5. The Nicolaitans are thus often associated more with a kind of license in lifestyle than with an early form of clericalism. For an example of this alternate interpretation, see G. R. Beasley-Murray, *Revelation*, The New Century Bible Commentary (1974, reprint, Grand Rapids: Eerdmans, 1983), 74.

4. John McClintock and James Strong, *Cyclopaedia of Biblical, Theological, and Ecclesiastical Literature* (New York: Harper and Brothers Publishers, 1870), 3:264.

5. Eddie Gibbs, *LeadershipNext: Changing Leaders in a Changing Culture* (Downers Grove, IL: InterVarsity Press, 2005), 33.

6. Jim is not his real name. The name was changed to protect the not so innocent.

7. Alan Hirsch and Debra Hirsch, *Untamed: Reactivating a Missional Form of Discipleship* (Grand Rapids: Baker Books, 2010), 74.

8. Dee Hock, "The Art of Chaordic Leadership," *Leader to Leader* 15 (Winter 2000): 20-26, www.hesselbeininstitute.org/knowledgecenter/ journal.aspx?ArticleID=62 (accessed June 14, 2012).

9. Ricketson, *Follower First*, 73.

10. Hock, "The Art of Chaordic Leadership."

11. Interview with author.

12. Not his real name.

13. Margaret J. Wheatley, *Leadership and the New Science: Discovering Order in a Chaotic World*, 2nd ed. (San Francisco: Berrett-Koehler Publishers, 1999), 24-25.

14. Kathy Escobar, *Down We Go: Living into the Wild Ways of Jesus* (Folsom, CA: Civitas Press, 2011), 151.

15. See Wheatley, *Leadership and the New Science*, 29.

16. Ibid., 43.

CHAPTER 3

1. Brennan Manning, *Abba's Child: The Cry of the Heart for Intimate Belonging*, rev. and expanded (Colorado Springs: NavPress, 2002), 34.

2. A. W. Tozer, *The Pursuit of God* (Harrisburg, PA: Christian Publications, 1948), 45.

3. Bill Kinnon, "Jesus and the Marlboro Man," *Kinnon.tv* (blog), November 27, 2011, http://kinnon.tv/2011/11/jesus-and-the-marlboro -man.html (accessed April 20, 2012).

4. Escobar, *Down We Go*, 33-34.

5. Sandy Hotchkiss, *Why Is It Always About You? The Seven Deadly Sins of Narcissism* (New York: Free Press, 2003), xi.

6. *Diagnostic and Statistical Manual of Mental Disorders*, 4th ed. (Washington, DC: American Psychiatric Association, 2000), 714-15.

7. John Emerich Edward Dalberg-Acton, 1st Baron Acton, "Letter to Bishop Mandell Creighton, April 5, 1887," in *Historical Essays and Studies*, ed. J. N. Figgis and R. V. Laurence (London: Macmillan, 1907).

8. C. S. Lewis, *Mere Christianity* (New York: Touchstone, 1996), 113.

9. Hotchkiss, *Why Is It Always About You?*, 142.

10. From an email message to author, September 2011.

11. See Hotchkiss, *Why Is It Always About You?*, 20.

12. Ibid.

13. See Ibid.

14. Manfred F. R. Kets de Vries, *Leaders, Fools, and Impostors: Essays on the Psychology of Leadership* (San Francisco: Jossey-Bass, 1993), 24.

15. Hotchkiss, *Why Is It Always About You?*, 146.

16. de Vries, *Leaders, Fools, and Impostors*, 11.

17. See Hotchkiss, *Why Is It Always About You?*, 24.

18. Interview by author with a former church staff member.

19. Eleanor D. Payson, *The Wizard of Oz and Other Narcissists: Coping with the One-Way Relationship in Work, Love, and Family* (Royal Oak, MI: Julian Day Publications, 2002), 8-9.

PART II—INTRODUCTION

1. Rob Lebow and Randy Spitzer, *Accountability: Freedom and Responsibility Without Control* (San Francisco: Berrett-Koehler, 2002), 7.

2. Robert K. Greenleaf, et al., *The Servant-Leader Within: A Transformative Path* (New York: Paulist Press, 2003), 1.

3. William Barclay, *We Have Seen the Lord!: The Passion and Resurrection of Jesus Christ* (Louisville, KY: Westminster John Knox Press, 1975), 9.

4. "Jazz Quotes," A Passion for Jazz, http://www.apassion4jazz.net/quotations5.html (accessed May 10, 2012).

CHAPTER 4

1. Søren Kierkegaard, *Works of Love: Some Christian Reflections in the Form of Discourses*, trans. Howard V. Hong and Edna H. Hong (New York: Harper, 1962), 68.

2. Kenneth Samuel Wuest, *Wuest's Word Studies from the Greek New Testament for the English Reader* (Grand Rapids: Eerdmans, 1973), 1:11.

3. Gilbert G. Bilezikian, *Community 101: Reclaiming the Church as Community of Oneness* (Grand Rapids: Zondervan Publishing House, 1997), 67.

4. Escobar, *Down We Go*, 155.

5. Bessenecker, *How to Inherit the Earth*, 15.

6. J. Oswald Sanders, *Spiritual Leadership: Principles of Excellence for Every Believer* (Chicago: Moody Press, 1994), 23.

7. John P. Dickson, *Humilitas: A Lost Key to Life, Love, and Leadership* (Grand Rapids: Zondervan, 2011), 24.

8. Daniel Goleman, *Emotional Intelligence* (New York: Bantam Books, 1995), 148.

9. Sanders, *Spiritual Leadership*, 21.

10. Albert Schweitzer and Antje Bultmann Lemke, *Out of My Life and Thought: An Autobiography*, 60th anniversary ed. (Baltimore: Johns Hopkins University Press, 2009), 88-89.

11. Jayakumar Christian, *God of the Empty-Handed: Poverty, Power, and the Kingdom of God* (Monrovia, CA: MARC, 1999), 165.

12. Ibid., 188-89.

13. Ibid., 197.

14. Lewis, *Mere Christianity*, 113-14.

15. Ibid., 114.

CHAPTER 5

1. Len Hjalmarson, "The Five-Fold Ministry and the Birth of New Movements," NextReformation.com, http://nextreformation.com/wp-admin/leadership/five-fold.htm (accessed April 24, 2012).

2. Wayne Alderson and Nancy Alderson McDonnell, *Theory R Management* (Nashville: Thomas Nelson Publishers, 1994), 174.

3. *Webster's New World Dictionary* (1986), s.v. "employee."

4. This is a true story, but Rob is not his real name.

5. David Fitch, "On How Flat Leadership Works for Mission: The Three Ps," *Reclaiming the Mission* (blog), June 15, 2010, http://www.reclaimingthemission.com/on-how-flat-leadership-works-for-mission-the-three-p-'s/ (accessed May 1, 2012). Used by permission.

6. Ibid.

7. Frank Viola, *Reimagining Church: Pursuing the Dream of Organic Christianity* (Colorado Springs: David C. Cook, 2008), 175.

8. Kellerman, *Followership*, 56-57.

9. Wheatley, *Leadership and the New Science*, 76.

10. Peter M. Senge, "Communities of Leaders and Learners," *Harvard Business Review*, 75th anniversary issue (September–October 1997): 30-32.

11. Alan Hirsch, *The Forgotten Ways: Reactivating the Missional Church* (Grand Rapids: Brazos Press, 2006), 19.

12. Peter Block, *Community: The Structure of Belonging* (San Francisco: Berrett-Koehler Publishers, 2008), 73.

13. Wheatley, *Leadership and the New Science*, 20.

14. Brennan Manning, *The Rabbi's Heartbeat* (Colorado Springs: NavPress, 2003), 38-39.

CHAPTER 6

1. Bill Easum, *Leadership on the Other Side: No Rules, Just Clues* (Nashville: Abingdon, 2000), 88.

2. Cole, *Organic Leadership*, 88.

3. In Rom. 13:1 the apostle Paul gives instructions regarding submission to civil authority.

4. Len Hjalmarson, "Kingdom Leadership in the Postmodern Era," NextReformation.com, http://nextreformation.com/wp-admin/resources/Leadership.pdf (accessed May 1, 2012).

5. Mike Bonem and Roger Patterson, *Leading from the Second Chair: Serving Your Church, Fulfilling Your Role, and Realizing Your Dreams* (San Francisco: Jossey-Bass, 2005), 1, 3.

6. Christina Baldwin, *The Circle Way: A Leader in Every Chair* (San Francisco: Berrett-Koehler Publishers, 2010), 10-11.

7. See Cole, *Organic Leadership*, 91.

8. George Cladis, *Leading the Team-Based Church: How Pastors and Church Staffs Can Grow Together into a Powerful Fellowship of Leaders* (San Francisco: Jossey-Bass, 1999), 39.

9. Paraphrased from Easum, *Leadership on the Other Side*, 144-42.

10. Viola, *Reimagining Church*, 207-8.

11. Paraphrased from Neil Cole, *Organic Leadership*, 77.

12. Ibid., 178.

CHAPTER 7

1. Keith Meyer, *Whole Life Transformation* (Downers Grove, IL: InterVarsity Press, 2010), 77.

2. Frederick Buechner, *The Magnificent Defeat* (New York: Harper-One, 1966), 100.

3. Nannerl Keohane, "On Leadership," *Perspectives on Politics* 3, no. 4 (December 2005): 715.

4. Dallas Willard, *The Divine Conspiracy* (San Francisco: Harper-SanFrancisco, 1997), 301.

5. Hirsch and Hirsch, *Untamed*, 25.

6. Will Vaus, *Mere Theology: A Guide to the Thought of C. S. Lewis* (Downers Grove, IL: InterVarsity Press, 2004), 167.

7. Paul Stanley and J. Robert Clinton, *Connecting: The Mentoring Relationships You Need to Succeed* (Colorado Springs: NavPress, 1992), 18.

UNLEADER—A BENEDICTION

1. Michael Polanyi, *Personal Knowledge: Towards a Post-Critical Philosophy* (London: Routledge and Kegan Paul, 1962), 56.

2. Ibid., 55.

3. The source of this story is unknown. It is found in several versions, often with different characters assuming the main roles, such as a rabbi and his servant. See "Driven to Succeed," Snopes.com, http://www.snopes.com/humor/jokes/chauffeur.asp (accessed May 11, 2012).

"An essential for anyone who desires to live out the mission of Jesus in their world."

—**Dan Kimball,** author, professor, and pastor at Vintage Faith Church in Santa Cruz

A 12-week guide for communities seeking to participate more fully in God's mission and better understand the foundations, principles, and practices of missional life.

MISSIONAL ESSENTIALS
A Guide for Experiencing
God's Mission in Your Life
By Brad Brisco & Lance Ford

"A must read for any ministry or organizational leader, first-time pastor, or seasoned veteran who is considering a new assignment, and an invaluable resource for any overseer of young pastors."
—David Busic, President of Nazarene Theological Seminary

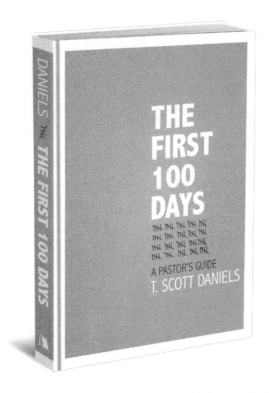

Every time a pastor goes to a new church, he or she forms hopes, dreams, and expectations—without necessarily realizing it—for the progress and growth of his or her new ministry. *The First 100 Days* provides guidance and insight for pastors to help them lead with godly wisdom and purpose during the first months of a new ministry.

The First 100 Days
A Pastor's Guide
T. Scott Daniels
ISBN 978-0-8341-2554-4

BEACON HILL PRESS
OF KANSAS CITY

www.BeaconHillBooks.com | 1.800.877.0700

Stay up to date on new releases,
and discuss *UnLeader*
and other Beacon Hill books:

[f] /BeaconHillPress

[t] @BeaconHillPress

[p] /BeaconHillPress

BEACON HILL PRESS
OF KANSAS CITY